An Odyssey Through The Dark

An Odyssey Through the Dark

REHAN RAZA

PRABHAT
PAPERBACKS

Published by

PRABHAT PAPERBACKS

An Imprint of Prabhat Prakashan Pvt. Ltd.
4/19 Asaf Ali Road,
New Delhi–110 002 (INDIA)
e-mail: prabhatbooks@gmail.com

ISBN 978-93-5521-190-3
AN ODYSSEY THROUGH THE DARK
by Rehan Raza

Edition
2022

Price
₹ 250 (Rupees Two Hundred Fifty Only)

Printed at
Japan Art, Delhi

Dedicated to

"The indefatigable covid warriors who served humanity in the direst of times and to those whom we lost on the way".

Author's Note

The pandemic that began in the year 2020 turned the world around in an unprecedented way, causing huge economic and social disruption and devastating millions of people. This story was conceived while I was engaged in Covid relief work as Sub Divisional Magistrate. At this crucial time, I was at the forefront of disaster management and had the onerous task of managing the pandemic situation and ensuring compliance of Covid protocols. When tales of pain and suffering were making headlines in the newspapers, I was witnessing them first-hand, ensuring necessary and timely help to people. The heart-rending chronicles of human suffering that I bore testimony to, were also stories of grit, determination and courage, that are the essence of human beings. *An Odyssey Through The Dark* was conceived during this time when I was sinking in the sea of human emotions while discharging my duty diligently.

It is a romantic love story interwoven around the incidents which happened in Delhi during the pandemic times. It is the narrative of a young man who with his grit, determination, selflessness and intelligence transforms challenges into opportunities. The story reflects how hard work and commitment can bring difference to an individual's life. It is also about human relationships and how people respond to challenging circumstances. The story is written as an exemplum of how one must conduct oneself through the ups and downs of life. The story captures a few real-life incidents which happened around that time. The inspiration for the characters and incidents in the story, therefore, came from the people and their real-life struggles in those difficult and trying times.

This book glorifies the virtues of friendship, sacrifice, love, affection, courage, conviction, and conscientiousness that are inherent in human beings.

❑

Acknowlegements

This book came into being out of real-life experiences that were both moving and rewarding. It was conceived while working at the immensely challenging task of containing and managing Covid-19 disease as an administrator. While the world was reeling under the mayhem unleashed by the Covid pandemic, the district administration was relentlessly working to provide help to the affected people and enforce order into the chaos. The inspiration came from all the people who worked in my team tirelessly, ceaselessly and also became model for the characters of this story.

This effort has become possible only with the help, support and motivation of many elders and friends.

First and foremost, my sincere and deep gratitude goes to my wife Nabeela Wali, who patiently and dauntlessly motivated me to perform my duty in the highly exigent circumstances. Her constant support, practical help, encouragement, and feedback during the writing process were indispensable. To my siblings, who have always been by my side, and motivated me to write this book.

I am thankful to Ms. Poonam Chaudhary, Ms. Namita Gupta, Ms. Ekta Verma, Ms. Yogita Arora, Sh. Sushil Gupta and Sh. Anoop for their tireless and creative contributions in the book.

My respected seniors—Sh. Vijay Kumar Dev, (IAS), Sh. Sanjeev Khirwar, (IAS), Sh. Ashish Kundra, (IAS), Sh. Ankur Garg, (IAS), Sh. S.B. Deepak Kumar, (IAS), Sh. Prince Dhawan, (IAS), Sh. Udit Prakash Rai, (IAS), Sh. Sandeep Mishra, (DANICS) and Sh. Awanish Kumar, (IAS)—have been a source of inspiration for me and their experiences and knowledge have helped me give this book the desired shape. I am also grateful to my District Magistrate Ms. Cheshta Yadav, (IAS) for constantly motivating and guiding me.

The efforts put in by Sh. Parveen Kumar, Sh. Joginder Rana, Ms. Madhu Soni, Ms. Samina Nesar, Ms. Albeena Wali, Sh. Sandeep Kumar, Sh. Ambikesh Mishra and Sh. Mohit Malik are appreciable and deserve due mention.

Efforts have been made to give credit where it is due for the material contained herein. If inadvertently I have missed giving due credit to anyone, future publications will do so upon bringing it to my attention.

❑

Contents

1

CHAPTER

The Breakdown

Crumbling is not an instant's Act
A fundamental pause
Dilapidation's processes
Are organised Decays.

—Emily Dickinson

Rahul's tearful eyes lay transfixed on Arun's face whose breathing was visibly shallow and troubled. Trapped in a PPE kit and looking at his dear friend's face through the veil of a face shield, Rahul felt a sudden instinct to pull down the physical barriers and hug his friend tight, and assure him that everything would soon be fine. Countless memories of the invaluable times that they had revelled in flashed through his eyes in those moments.

His reverie was broken by a tap on his shoulder. As he tried to blink away a tear at the corner of his eye, Aditi gently nudged him to move out of the ICU. He resignedly followed her into the doffing room. It took them a while to get out of their PPE kits and change into normal clothes. The coronavirus pandemic had added gobs of rituals to a common person's day and more so to a person in the vicinity of a COVID-positive patient. The word positive had also taken very negative connotations during the pandemic. It was ironic, because at the same time the epidemic had enriched Rahul's life with experiences, challenges and opportunities as well. He had always used the proverbial lemons which life threw his way to make lemonade. But with his childhood buddy struggling for life, Rahul was disconsolate and had lost his ability to look at anything positively.

His blossoming romance with Aditi had also hit a rough patch. There was an indescribable distance between them. The extraneous time needed for even the simplest of chores, long working hours, management of their individual professions and commitments, and the tedious task of following the COVID protocols even when they were alone had not just made them distant but also taken away the charm of their relationship. Perennial tiredness and separation from their families were taking a toll on their psychological health, and they realised it too. They continued being together in the hope that they would be able to sail through the storm together.

Rahul's phone buzzed and without looking at the name flashing on the screen, he picked up the call. It was Anjali, Arun's girlfriend, on the other end. Rahul felt an irrepressible need to blurt out what he had been dreading, that his worst fear might come true. He composed himself before responding. He told Anjali that Arun was under the observation of doctors and the situation was under control. They just needed Remdesivir, a life-saving drug, which was not available over-the-counter in the market, to help Arun's symptoms. During the surge of the COVID pandemic, its export had been banned. However, with a fall in the number of cases— below 30,000 per day across India—the government had again allowed its export. But now that this even deadlier, second wave of COVID-19 was prevailing, restrictions had again been imposed on its export. Despite these restrictions, the drug was not easily available in the market for the patients. People were ready to pay whatever they could to get it; demand was astronomically enhanced, along with delayed supplies and distributors resorting to hoarding and stockpiling as reported in the media. Rahul did not want to explain all these details to Anjali and upset her. He simply told her that Aditi was arranging for the drug and Arun should be fine as soon as Remdesivir was administered. He assured her that he would keep her updated and disconnected the line.

As he hung up the call, his phone buzzed again. It was Balvinder Singh. Rahul was expecting his call. He heard Balvinder Singh's words, "Rahul Beta, how is Arun?"

Rahul replied, "Not good, sir. He's still in the ICU. I am very scared. I don't know what to do. Our hopes are pinned on Remdesivir. Aditi is trying to get in touch with the authorities in district administration to get it as soon as possible. But in the meantime, there is no improvement in his health. I feel so helpless; I can't do anything except for relying on Aditi's abilities to get the medicine."

Balvinder Singh said, "Baba ji will see that all is well. Don't panic. You are a braveheart, boy. I remember how you and Arun took care of me when I was admitted to the hospital." He further added, "You also have to attend a meeting with Mr Bajaj regarding the supply of sanitisers and masks. Will you be able to make it?"

Rahul was flustered but replied in a calm tone, "Yes, sir. I have to go there but I am also concerned about leaving Arun alone."

Balvinder Singh said compassionately, "The meeting can be fixed for a later time. Do whatever you think is the need of the hour. Just go with your instincts."

Rahul felt relieved and assured him that he would try his best to meet Mr Bajaj and disconnected the call.

Aditi saw how agonised Rahul was. She was taciturn and kept walking by his side. She too knew it was not the right time to dwell on what had happened in the past few days. Rahul and Aditi needed to ponder over their relationship and weigh up its future. Meanwhile, they reached her room.

Aditi carefully sanitised her stethoscope and placed it in the drawer. She kept her eyes low in the hope that Rahul would start the conversation. Rahul, on the other hand, was dreading the onslaught of Aditi's questions and his own justifications that would follow if he said anything. Aditi easily perceived his doubts and discerned that she would have to address the elephant in the room. Rahul also realised the same and decided not to shy away from the discussion. They turned towards each other and started speaking at the same time. Aditi stopped speaking and gestured to Rahul to continue. He told Aditi in very clear words that he could not leave Arun's side to attend the meeting scheduled with Mr Bajaj for the afternoon.

Aditi already had these misgivings. But now, as those words fell on her ears, she felt a lump rising in her throat and a burst of anger, all at once. The fatigue of it all; the strenuous work in the hospital, strained relations with Rahul, and her own inadequacy in dealing with the medical crisis grew upon her. She was on the verge of breaking down. She wanted Rahul to trust her, to believe that she would arrange Remdesivir soon. She wanted Rahul to show faith in her ability and attend the meeting calmly, without worrying about Arun. But she could not put her expectations into words and what she did instead was push Rahul away with a sudden movement. Next, she heard her own rancorous words,

"Do as you please. I have nothing left to say, Rahul."

She stomped away with an air of finality and slammed the door behind her. Of late, they had been arguing incessantly. Neither felt loved or cared for. Earlier, they would understand each other's feelings without the use of words. But now even mountains of words could not bridge the vast gap that was creating a deep chasm in their relationship.

Rahul sat down with a thud as if he had no strength left in his body. He had never felt so powerless in his life. Life was playing some evil tricks on him. He was losing the two closest persons in his life. The city that gave him dreams and hopes had suddenly turned malefic. Arun, his buddy, his dear friend and confidante who stood with him like a rock in all situations, was fighting for his life; while Aditi, who came like a breath of fresh air in his life just a few months back, was drifting away from him. His world was collapsing. His spirits were broken and as he tried to raise himself, he sank into the chair again. He knew he was reeling from the finale of his relationship with Aditi but didn't want to end it. His bodily reactions and emotions were in a tangle. He was in love, and she was in love, but both of them were angry and confused. Simultaneously, he was hoping that things would work out with Aditi who had just walked away abruptly. He was in the throes of such a situation.

Amma's face was floating before his eyes. If only she was there with him, he would have buried his head in her lap. Her gentle touch would have dispersed those clouds of sorrow. A mother is like a song of comfort. How could Aditi expect him to leave Arun's side in this hour of dire need? A dejected Rahul could not comprehend it.

Rahul always felt that he had all the solutions. He was always sure of himself. It was not that he had not faced challenges in his life. The circumstances from which he had raised himself were never conducive if not hostile. He was a self-made man who had struggled his way up from being an unsophisticated small-town boy to a successful entrepreneur in a metropolitan city. It was Arun, his dear friend, who was there by his side at each step of the way when he was ascending the ladder of success. Now that Arun's life was fading with every passing moment, Rahul was not left with the strength to fight back. Life had dealt him a bad hand this time.

Rahul finally got up and started walking towards the elevator, oblivious of the flurry of nurses and doctors around him fighting an impossible battle. His mind was filled with thoughts of the time that he had spent with Arun in his village. The doors of the elevator opened and Rahul entered dazedly. His thoughts wandered down the lanes of his village, Mohammadpur, where he and Arun used to play, without a care in the world. They spent their boyhood in the tranquillity of that small village until Arun moved to Delhi when his father got settled there. Rahul was heartbroken when Arun left, but with time he had learnt to live without him.

The elevator doors dragged open and Rahul involuntarily walked out towards the exit. A woman was wailing in the corridor for her husband who had just died of COVID. Heart-rending cries echoed in the corridor. They fell on Rahul's ears too but to no avail. He kept walking subconsciously, feeling numb. The cries for oxygen, death wails and desperate squeals for help were all that one heard, day and night in that gloomy domain. Daylight fell upon his face as he came out of the dimly lit hospital compound into the waiting area. The sounds of wailing trailed away.

Hardly had he come out when he received Aditi's call. What could be the matter now? Rahul was both exhausted and irritated, perhaps at his own ineptitude to handle the situation. With the slow movements that mirrored the mental state of a person who has yielded himself to fate after a lost fight, he answered the call. Aditi spoke in a matter-of-fact way, but he could not hear her properly amidst the din of the waiting area. Aditi repeated slowly.

"Listen carefully, Rahul. I just received a call from the district office. They have been able to arrange Remdesivir injections and Dr Ehsan has promised to get them delivered at the hospital itself. Please coordinate with him and bring them to me at the earliest." Aditi's voice was cold and distant.

Rahul didn't know how to react. He was ecstatic as Remdesivir had been arranged but at the same time, the complete indifference and coldness in Aditi's tone did not fail to register on Rahul. The weight of a crumbling relationship and dying friendship was too much to bear.

All of a sudden, Rahul felt that all the strength was drained out of his body. He collapsed on a nearby concrete bench. He felt he was not even a shadow of his former self who could rise up to any situation. The deadly pandemic that rose and fell erratically, the indifferent city that described its dead as mere numbers, his relationship that failed the test of time, all had broken his spirit completely. He needed to reconnect with himself. He looked up as if searching for a way to find himself again. The bright sunlight hurt his eyes as he looked towards the sky. Memories of the past days began flitting before his eyes. He remembered the day when he first stepped into the city of his dreams that had now turned into a nightmare. His memories harked him back to that fateful day when Arun had called him to Delhi in the month of December.

❑

2
CHAPTER

Setting Sail

There are only the pursued, the pursuing,
the busy, and the tired.

—F Scott Fitzgerald

"In Delhi, you will save way more than what you are even earning back there."

The words were ringing in Rahul's ears—words that held a promise of better days for him. He was experiencing an inexplicable thrill at the mere thought of that offer. The excitement was hard to control.

Rahul was swooping down the kutcha road of the village on his bicycle. He was desperate to tell Baba about his friend Arun's call. His sweat-soaked shirt and parched throat on a cold December afternoon could not beat his unabashed spirit. The five hundred metres that lay ahead of him seemed trivial, compared to the four kilometres that he had covered in the last ten minutes in his overzealous frenzy to reach home and share with his family the wonderful offer he had just received from Arun.

Though an avid tea-lover, he did not bother to even wave at his friends as he sped past the tea shop where he generally had his simmering evening cup of tea tempered with the discussions and comments on anything and everything under the sun. His brawny and sinewy appearance belied the sharp intellect and deep insight that he held, based not on his fancy but solid facts. His friends revered his judgements as he was a voracious reader and devoured every news article or book that came his way. He was the proverbial Guru who had a solution to every problem.

Rahul was a resident of Mohammadpur—a small village within the ambit of the holy land of Gaya watered by the Phalgu River. The quaint village of Mohammadpur is about half a kilometre off the paved road that leads to the city of Gaya distancing thirty kilometres. The village was blessed with nature's bounty and surrounded by old trees and thickets inhabited by many species of animals and birds. People here lived a simple life away from the hustle and bustle of the cities. But as the times were changing, people were moving to greener pastures. Leaving their roots behind, they were now shifting to cities for better avenues.

The winter mornings in Gaya can kindle the poet in the most laconic of people. The easterly winds resonate with the sweet chirping sounds of morning birds. The veil of mist that blankets the city during the cold winter nights slowly dissipates as the city warms up in anticipation of the hustle and bustle of another day. The day begins with the holy tintinnabulation of temple bells and chanting of mantras as the whiff of incense rises in the air.

Rahul belonged to this quiet universe where life moved at a leisurely pace and the parameters of being successful were simple and few. But his ambitions were inconsistent with this cracker-barrel life. He wished to prove himself beyond the boundaries of his village. All that he waited for was an opportunity. Arun opened this door for him when he told him about the opening in his office.

Rahul had reached the paved road of the village as he was pedalling frantically. Rahul was a bright and promising boy in the village with a Master's degree in Mathematics. He turned 23 this month only. Due to the poor economic condition of his family, he had to start earning while he was still studying. Rahul began working as a data entry operator at a pharmacy shop during the day at Khizersarai, 7 kilometres away from the village. In the evenings, he would give tuition classes to the village children. But he was never the one to complain. Where other boys of his age would think of owning a new pair of jeans while glancing over the photos of actors in the magazines in the tea shop, Rahul would be reading the editorials and other informative articles in the newspapers. At other times, he would be seen scanning the *Employment News*. Such was Rahul, never wasting his time on trivialities. After all, he had to take care of his family of six—Amma, Baba, two sisters and a younger brother. Rahul, always the sensible and responsible one, was a guide to Reema, Sugna and Pintu, his siblings.

Rahul's sister Reema was going to turn 24 that year. Doe-eyed Reema was considered a village belle. Their parents were looking for a suitable match for her. But they were not able to arrange for a hefty amount of 3 or 4 lakh rupees for dowry. For the last two years, they had been looking for a suitable groom for her. But whenever things progressed, the big question of dowry arose and things could not materialise. No one agreed to a dowry of less than 3 or 4 lakhs. This excluded the wedding jewellery and other expenses. The stooping shoulders of his parents with dwindling resources could not afford such hefty expenditure.

His father, Mewaram, worked at the shop of a village merchant,with five kaththas of agricultural land and a total deposit of Rs 50,000 as his assets. Mewaram toiled his whole life for his family. The land that he had was not sufficient to sustain them, so he had to do other jobs to make his living. Although with his meagre income he could not dream of a lavish life, nevertheless, he had managed to provide a decent education to his children. He was a simple and hard-working man and these values were the only legacy that he could leave to his children. He had high hopes from Rahul as he had seen the same honesty and assiduousness in him as he himself had strived to practice all his life. Rahul was sensible and had his head firmly on his shoulders. He was never daunted by difficult situations.

It was a cold winter afternoon when Rahul received a call from his dear friend Arun. Rahul was wrapping up his work for the day when his phone buzzed.

"Hello Rahul, Arun this side. How are you?"

"Hey, Arun! I am good. How are you, brother? It's been a long time since we talked," Rahul replied gleefully. He was exulted to hear his close friend's voice after such a long time.

"I am good too. How is everyone at home?" Arun asked.

"The usual struggles of life are going on."

"Did you find any suitable match for Reema Didi?" Arun asked.

"Not yet, brother. Dowry is the biggest obstacle. Don't know how hard I would need to work to match up to the expectations of a good family!" He replied despondently.

"Don't get disappointed, brother. Something will work out soon. Listen, I have an exciting opportunity for you here in Delhi." Arun was sounding thrilled and told Rahul about a new opening in his office. Rahul fitted the bill and Arun had some clout with his boss. The job was Rahul's for the taking. The salary was handsome too. Arun himself was earning forty-five thousand a month. No one knew of Rahul's capabilities and diligent nature better than Arun. After all, the two were childhood buddies, who had studied in the same class, and were inseparable. Arun told Rahul that his boss needed an honest and reliable data entry operator at the earliest and he had published advertisements in many places for the post. So this was not an opportunity to be missed.

Rahul was initially puzzled by this sudden development.

"Uhh... Arun. Thank you, brother, for being so concerned, but how will I manage in a big city like Delhi? I have never been there and know nothing of the workings of a city like Delhi. And what about my family? Everyone's responsibility is on my shoulders." Rahul expressed his concerns. He was in a dilemma. He was filled with joy on getting this opportunity, but he was also worried and anxious at the prospect of moving away from his family.

"You won't be alone, Rahul. You can stay with me. Think it over, you will get to earn more and also save for your family. You can easily arrange for Reema Didi's wedding expenses. In Delhi, you will save more than what you are earning back there. Besides, you could be promoted sooner than later if you work hard and diligently. The promotion and increment scene here is quite good," Arun spoke in a persuasive manner. Rahul assured Arun that he would revert by the next day and hung up the call.

The cogent arguments of Arun bore fruit and succeeded in convincing an uncertain Rahul. As the advantageousness of the offer sank in, his eyes gleamed at the thought of the new opportunity knocking at his door. Now he would be able to marry off his sister in a decent way. And their house too could be repaired after all these years of neglect. After this conversation with Arun, Rahul felt as if his world was going to change forever. He couldn't wait to reach home and tell Amma and Baba about it all. A job in Delhi! He was thrilled at the prospect. In his present circumstances, he made a meagre 3,000 rupees after toiling for the whole day. An MSc in Mathematics, he was an intelligent and brilliant lad bound to his responsibilities by a grim fate. He didn't want to miss this opportunity.

Rahul made up his mind after brooding over it for a moment. If not now, then when? Only Amma and Baba's consent was needed. Why would anyone reject an offer like that? What was not there in it? Everything was sorted, even the accommodation. Arun told him that he could stay at his paying guest accommodation at a monthly rent of four thousand rupees. Other expenses would be around two to three thousand. In this way, he could save a decent amount.

Rahul got down from his bicycle and parked it on the porch, still preoccupied with the thoughts of leaving for Delhi. The sun had already set by now. Darkness reigned everywhere but his heart was illuminated with a new ray of hope.

Their house was an old and ramshackle structure badly in need of repair. Mewaram's paltry earnings could not make room for such expenses in all these years.

Rahul went inside the house calling Reema, "Didi... Didi"...

Reema was busy with the dinner preparation in the kitchen. Rahul sat a few feet away from the stove and excitedly told Reema, "Didi, one good news for us. Tomorrow, I am going to Delhi."

Reema knew very well that Rahul was quick to take decisions. All these years whenever he had come up and thrown one-liners like that, he had meant it each time. But on this occasion, even Reema was caught off guard. She exclaimed, "What? Delhi! Are you crazy! Do you even know how far that is? It takes a whole day on a train to travel and reach there."

Rahul rhapsodically narrated the conversation that he had with Arun.

"This is a great opportunity, Didi! Imagine twenty-five thousand rupees per month! All our miseries can end soon if I go there. If I save even ten thousand per month, I can still have a saving of one lakh twenty thousand in one year. I will be able to arrange money for your marriage too," said Rahul, teasing Reema who blushed at the thought of getting married.

"But without any plans? You have never been to Delhi before. How will you manage alone in Delhi, Bhai?" Reema expressed her concern. But in her heart, she was glad for Rahul who sounded like an over excited child.

While Reema and Rahul were talking, Sugna, his younger sister, came to the kitchen with Amma following behind.

"The brother-sister duo seems to be having an important discussion going on here. You sound very excited, Rahul," Amma said as she stood in the doorway.

Rahul quickly told her about his talk with Arun.

"Stop joking with your poor mother," Amma said in disbelief.

Rahul told her everything about the job and other prospects to allay her doubts and fears.

"And where will you stay in such a big city?" Amma asked a little seriously.

"Amma, don't you worry! Arun is living in the hostel where he will make arrangements for me to stay too. I will manage," said Rahul.

"Look at Arun, he is earning a handsome salary and is able to manage all expenses of the house. His sister's wedding is also fixed for next year. It all happened because he is working in Delhi. I'll never be able to make it big if I don't take this step." Rahul made a case for himself.

"Now what can I say if you have decided." Amma acquiesced. Her concern was not about his job or where he would stay. She could not bring herself to accept the fact that her dear son, who had been around all these years, would live away from her now. Rahul knew that Amma would be fine as soon as the news sank in.

There was silence for a while. Pintu, who was loitering around, pitched in, "Amma, he is right. If he is settled in Delhi, I will also get an opportunity for higher studies in Delhi University."

Amma was torn between letting Rahul go to make a name for himself, and not having the heart to let him go so far away from herself. Just then, the sound of an approaching bicycle was heard outside the house. Sugna ran out and returned to inform them that Baba had arrived. Baba was the voice of reason in the house. A man of few words, he did not take long to seal the deal. Rahul was elated. He was overcome with emotions as he touched Baba's feet for his blessings.

Rahul went in and started packing for the journey. Amma and Didi went on with cooking dinner as well as making *mathis* and *puris* for his journey. Rahul was both anxious as well as excited about this new development. Though Arun was a dear friend, deep in the recesses of his heart lay resentment, perhaps against his own stars, at the way he did not get the opportunities to advance himself in the world despite having it all in him. Arun on the other hand was lucky. Rahul was lost in these thoughts as he folded his shirt and mumbled to himself, "I will prove now and show everyone my worth".

****

The next day, Rahul took a bus to reach the station at around 12:30 p.m. He hurried to the ticket counter. There were about ten people at the general ticket counter and Rahul had to wait in the queue. It took him ten minutes to reach the ticket window. He quickly collected his ticket and ran towards platform number 1 to board the train.

The platform was crowded with passengers, vendors and vagabonds. You could buy bracelets, batteries, a new wallet or mouthwash, a comb or a set of headphones, and purchase food ranging from fruits to hard boiled eggs, from water and colas to chocolates and candies, from varieties of chaats to deep fried bread pakodas. Mahabodhi Express, the train that was taking Rahul to the city of his dreams, was expected to reach Delhi after a journey of about 16 hours.

Rahul was nonplussed to see the crowd at the entry gates of the two general compartments. Passengers were pushing and jostling each other to board the train. He somehow managed to enter the coach, but had to settle in a corner for lack of space.

It was 7:00 a.m. The train was running four hours behind schedule. It halted after five minutes before entering Ghaziabad. There was a sudden commotion of people in the train's general compartment. The vendors started boarding the train selling hot tea and coffee, Frooti, potato chips, bread rolls, popcorn and other sundry items. People who had slept adjacent to each other through the night, in the overcrowded general coach were now awake. Rahul had spent the entire night sitting on a newspaper, cramped in a corner. He had been on his guard throughout the night, never letting go of the backpack that he was carrying.

The train was about to reach Ghaziabad junction. A large number of working-class people native to Bihar, usually engaged as daily wage labourers living in Delhi and NCR, travelled by this train. As the train halted at platform number 2, more than half of the passengers of the general compartment deboarded the coach. The ordeal of the journey was a bummer for Rahul. The entire experience was a nightmare. For the first time after boarding the train, he was able to move his hands freely. He slowly stood up and stretched himself, trying to overcome the fatigue of the journey. Rubbing his eyes, he looked out of the train.

An elderly man sitting on his berth, signalled Rahul to sit with him. Rahul was tired of sitting on the floor, so he took the offer ecstatically. After a few minutes of silence, the elderly man struck up a conversation with him and asked where he was from.

As the interaction between the two of them developed, Uncle ji started talking about his family. "My son is a manager in a private company. He is married to a teacher and has a 12-year- old son and a 5-year-old daughter. The entire family lives in Ashok Vihar. I am going to meet my grandchildren. I will stay there for a week. My wife couldn't travel because of her arthritic pain. But she wanted to send these *gond laddoos* for our grandchildren. They are very healthy and help to improve stamina and build immunity. I couldn't refuse her wish. So I came without her. I generally don't travel without her." Uncle ji affectionately shared all his details in one breath. It is not surprising to find such hail-fellow-well-met kind of people in Indian trains.

"Why are you going to Delhi, Beta?" Uncle ji inquired further. Rahul was sceptical of being too comfortable with strangers, so he shared only a few details about the purpose of his journey.

Uncle ji, undeterred, kept up a spirited conversation with Rahul. The train had crossed the Yamuna bridge. Again, there was a flurry of activity in the compartment. People started to pack their belongings. Uncle ji also started packing. Rahul had only one backpack, so he did not worry much and was enjoying the sights outside the train.

After about 20 minutes, the train stopped at platform number 6 of New Delhi Railway Station. People started deboarding the train. Uncle ji and Rahul waited for their turn to deboard. Meanwhile, the old man informed his son about the arrival of the train. As he finished talking on the phone, Rahul asked Uncle ji if he could use his phone to make a call to his friend. Uncle ji gladly conceded.

Arun picked up the phone in one ring. He asked Rahul to take a bus and come to Patel Chest Chowk, and then ask the tea seller at the corner tea shop for directions to Goyal House. After finishing the conversation, Rahul returned the phone to Uncle ji. As Uncle ji was trying to lift his heavy bag, Rahul courteously took his bag and carried it effortlessly.

When Uncle ji tried to alight from the train onto the platform, he couldn't find a firm footing on the ground and his ankle twisted. A sharp cry of pain involuntarily escaped his mouth and he fell down even as he tried to find something to hold on to for support. Rahul exclaimed and immediately supported Uncle ji with extreme care and helped him sit on a nearby bench. He was suddenly aware of the frailness of Uncle ji's frame and couldn't help but think how he would have held his own father in such a situation.

Rahul called Uncle ji's son Akshat and told him about the mishap. Akshat, who was waiting outside impatiently, was astounded. He had an important meeting to attend and he didn't want to be late. This unwanted delay distressed him beyond measure. He quickly parked his scooter and came inside. Uncle ji glanced at his son's face and one look revealed the extreme annoyance and irritation that his son was trying to hide. This realisation that his own son was annoyed by the situation was enough for him to feel apologetic at being the reason for his dismay. He simply sat there with downcast eyes.

Akshat asked Rahul to help his father and hastily thrust a 2000-rupee note into his palm to take care of the expenses. He stormed out of the station without waiting for any reply. A score of people had gathered around them to enjoy the spectacle. Uncle ji and Rahul were both new to the city. Rahul had no clue where to take Uncle ji. He was unnerved by this sudden happening. And his simple heart failed to understand how a son could abandon his father like that.

Rahul's sympathy was with the injured and dejected father. So he called up his friend Arun and narrated the whole incident to him. Arun advised him to hire an auto rickshaw to City Hospital, where he knew one peon, who was from his village. Uncle ji was experiencing excruciating pain and was unable to take a single step. Rahul had to do some quick thinking. He asked a porter to carry the bags. He easily lifted Uncle ji and came out of the station looking for an auto rickshaw. Luckily for him, the first auto rickshaw he saw agreed to take them to City Hospital. He thanked the porter and gave him 50 rupees and asked the driver to hurry up. They reached the hospital a quarter of an hour later.

Uncle ji was immediately taken to the emergency room, and Rahul was informed that Uncle ji had fractured his ankle and the complex procedure would require him to be admitted and undergo a surgery. They needed the consent form to be signed by a relative. Rahul tried to negotiate with the receptionist and explained his position to her. She asked him to shift the patient to another hospital since she could not overlook the administrative formalities. Rahul helplessly looked around when he saw a young lady doctor walk out from the OPD.

She was the first and perhaps the most beautiful woman Rahul's eyes beheld since he stepped into the city. Her large dark eyes were giving tough competition to her dark and dense mane. Her face looked like it was sculpted out of white marble by Pygmalion himself. Rahul was drawn towards her, irrespective of himself.

Dr Aditi was a junior resident doctor at the hospital. She was preparing for her Post Graduate NEET examination. A bright student with an empathetic attitude towards people, she always lived up to the challenging situations her noble profession demanded.

Rahul felt an unexplained impulse to seek help from her. He blurted out the situation as it was and begged her to help him in getting Uncle ji the required treatment. He told her how Uncle ji was injured, how his son had left them at the station and how on his first day in Delhi he was in a hospital with a stranger and didn't know what to do. Rahul's simplicity and selfless nature left a mark on Dr Aditi. He seemed to be a very naive and simple young man and Aditi wondered if he was just faking it to get the old man the necessary treatment.

Leaving her doubts aside, Dr Aditi focused on helping the old man. She signed the medical form and asked the receptionist to call for the orthopaedic doctor on duty. Within a few minutes, Uncle ji was wheeled into the minor OT room. It took the doctor an hour to perform the procedure. Ultimately, he was brought out of the minor OT and shifted to a general ward.

Rahul was overwhelmed with her kind gesture and expressed his gratitude towards Dr Aditi. Rahul called Akshat and told him that he was at City Hospital in Ashok Vihar.

When Akshat reached the hospital, he couldn't thank Rahul enough. Uncle ji could now properly introduce Rahul to his son. After putting his father's luggage in the car, he got an auto rickshaw for Rahul. He instructed the auto driver to take Rahul to Patel Chest Chowk and also settled the fare in advance. Akshat was embarrassed at what had transpired between him and his father earlier in the day and even more so by the fact that Rahul was a witness to it all. He had no explanation for his behaviour and so remained silent over it. But inwardly, he realised that he was so caught up with the demands of his office work that he couldn't even find the time to care for his father who was in need. This gesture towards Rahul was his way of dealing with his own embarrassment and making up for what Rahul had to go through.

Akshat shared his mobile number with Rahul, in case he needed any assistance. Rahul sat in the auto and thanked Akshat. On reaching Goyal House, Rahul saw a wall clock hanging in front of the stairs. It was 10 p.m. As he pressed the doorbell, he heard someone call Arun, "Arun Bhai! It must be your friend you have been so anxiously waiting for".

Arun rushed to open the door. "Rahul! I have been so worried about you. Was your journey comfortable? How was the experience at the hospital? Did you face any difficulty in reaching here?" He fired a volley of questions at him and hugged him without waiting for an answer.

Arun took Rahul into his room. He asked him to freshen up and take some rest. Since it was already very late, Arun said that he would take Rahul to his office the next day. Meanwhile, he asked the cook, Harilal, to prepare ginger tea for Rahul. Ginger tea is a staple in Indian homes. It is invigorating and relieves all the pressure and stress of the day. Rahul took a sip of the piping hot tea and said, "Aahaha, Arun, nothing in this world can beat this ginger tea!"

Arun, taking a sip and gulping it down, said, "Yes, Rahul. Your Amma makes the best tea in this world." Rahul's corner of the eye filled with tears. "Haan, Amma's tea is everyone's favourite."

While they were talking, the other boys of the hostel gathered in the common room. One of them said, "Arun Bhai, introduce your friend to us."

Arun said, "He is my childhood friend, Rahul. We did our schooling together. He has come here for an interview in my office. I will take him to the office tomorrow. And Rahul, this is Manjeet. You have already met him. This is Manish, very naughty" and laughed, "but a sincere young boy. This is Ravi sir, he runs an NGO." He paused and said, "Look, here comes the most studious boy of our PG, Ankur. He is very intelligent. He is preparing for Civil Services and other entrance exams."

Rahul got up and shook hands with everyone. He smiled and said, "I am Rahul. I am here to try my luck in this city of dreams. Ankur Bhaiya and Ravi ji, you can call me anytime for support. Manish, Arun told me about your jokes. We will together make everyone laugh. I hope I will muck in with you all." All the boys hugged Rahul.

Meanwhile the cook had laid the dinner. They all enjoyed it. At the table they gossiped, laughed and shared their day's experience. Arun told them about how Rahul had helped Uncle ji at the railway station and gotten him medical treatment on his first day in the city. They were amazed at Rahul's quick thinking and helpful nature. All of them retired to their rooms after that.

Rahul, who was very tired, closed his eyes and slept instantaneously. A long journey was to be traversed by him.

****

The next day, Rahul reached Arun's office for the interview well in time. Arun introduced Rahul to his boss, Mr Balvinder Singh. He was a Punjabi quinquagenarian, a fair, broad-shouldered, burly man with thick, bushy moustaches and beard. He wore a big blue turban and the buttons of his crisp white shirt strained over his potbelly in an unsightly manner. He was well-settled in his life and accustomed to the workings of the world around him. He was of an unsuspecting disposition though, and this trusting nature had won him dedicated and loyal employees like Arun who often went out of their way to do things for him. Balvinder was a practical man who had worked hard on establishing his business in the position that it was in at that time. He had inherited these traits of industriousness and ingenuity from his father who had migrated to Delhi from Rawalpindi in 1947 after the partition of India, and built everything anew with sheer hard work and determination. Today, Balvinder had a decent house in Kamala Nagar and a profitable business providing employment to scores of people.

He commanded the office boy, "Oye Rakesh... Thoda chai coffee le aa kuchh."

Saying this, he signalled to Rahul to sit on the chair. Balvinder Singh asked Rahul about his education and work experience. After being satisfied with Rahul's credentials, he turned towards Arun and said, "Arun, after office hours, go and buy a smartphone for him. He seems to be a hard-working and sharp-minded fellow. *Aaj se hi isko kuchh kaam bata do, dhire dhire karta rahega*."

Emerging out of the boss's cabin, Arun hugged Rahul and held his hand. He showed him to his desk. Arun and Rahul began to work on the computer regarding some new orders.

At 6 o'clock in the evening, the office was closed. The boss had already left the office at 5 p.m. telling Arun that he had to attend a party.

Arun asked Rahul, "So how do you find the work here?"

Rahul replied, "Good. It was the first day. But I was totally jaded today. Feeling drained out." Arun smiled and said, "Chal, let's go to Chandni Chowk and unwind ourselves with jalebi and delicious parathas."

Rahul was amazed to see the market and its renovation process. He was truly enchanted by the many faces of the city. As he lay in his bed at night, he reflected on the past two days. He had never imagined a place to be full of so many different kinds of people and experiences. It seemed to him as if in a short span of time, he had seen the world. He, like other people from small towns, had considered that life in a city would be almost equal to heaven, wonderful and enjoyable. And within a few days, he had come across a dear friend, a helpless elderly man, a considerate doctor and a passionate employer. New ventures, experiments and socialising happen in cities and he said to himself, "Welcome Rahul, now grease your wheels and buckle up. It's time to show this city who has landed ashore this time." He closed his eyes, and a smile spread across his face.

❑

3

CHAPTER

Love Comes Knocking

He feeds upon her face by day and night,
And she with true kind eyes looks back on him,
Fair as the moon and joyful as the light.

—Christina Rossetti

It had been almost two months since Rahul left his village. His desires had taken wings. He had begun to soar high.

All his hard work had surely put him in the good books of his master. With a handsome salary every month and a diverse set of friends to keep him company, Rahul was finally finding his feet in the city. He had started living a life that he only dreamt of earlier. But still he was far from settling in the comfort of this contentment. He wanted to accomplish more in life and the job at Balvinder's publishing house was a stepping stone towards the future that he was envisioning for himself.

One fine Saturday morning in the month of February, the sun was coming out and the warmth was causing the smog to disappear slowly. Rahul woke up to the usual morning din of the city. Sweepers sweeping the streets, shutters rolling up, honking of bikes and scooters, all of this was new to Rahul. Back in his village, he would wake up to a medley of sounds of sparrows, teals, crows, quails, mynas and geese. But in big cities, it is hard to spot birds other than pigeons. Lazily walking out to the balcony, he pulled out a chair and decided to soak in the warm morning sun.

He picked up *The Hindu* and started skimming it. The newspaper was filled with reports on elections, riots, Donald Trump's visit to India and a plethora of information. Sitting in Delhi was like sitting at the epicentre of all political activities in India. Rahul still had not got over the feeling of being in a different world compared to his quiet existence in Mohammadpur.

He was engrossed in the newspaper, when he suddenly caught a glimpse of the two girls in the balcony of Tulip hostel across the street.

They were leaning on the balcony railing with coffee mugs in their hands. One of them was wearing an indigo pair of tights and a pink sweatshirt that highlighted her rosy cheeks. The other petite one was wearing a loose white pullover and black track pants. Her luminescent black eyes and prominent cheekbones enhanced her sun-kissed oval face. Her thick, black, waist-length hair that fell along her gym-toned body accentuated her golden complexion. Rahul was transfixed. He had seen such girls only in movies. He was trying to focus on his newspaper but could not stop himself from stealing a glance at them. Not because he was attracted towards them but only because they looked so much different than the girls he had seen back home, who were always dressed in suits with dupattas over their heads. He was still trying to assimilate the city culture where girls intermingled freely with boys, discussed and debated current affairs and policy matters, and called each other buddies.

In the Indian villages, even today, women are judged by their dressing style and way of talking. The Western style of dressing is considered a manifestation of immoral conduct on the part of women. But in a big city like Delhi, it is common and socially acceptable. The rural–urban divide exists not only in the economic equations but also in terms of social mores.

Tulip hostel, which was right across the street, was a paying guest accommodation for girls. Patel Chest is a hub of paying guest houses which provide living quarters to scores of young men and women who either pursue university education or prepare for various competitive exams. Many young aspirants migrate to metropolitan cities in the hope of making it big. These homestays are like sanctuaries which house youth migrating to the cities in search of better pastures. In the same way as the migratory birds travel thousands of miles to places where they can find better habitat and ecological conditions, Rahul was one among many who found a sanctuary here to carve a niche for himself.

Rahul was staring in amazement at the girls from behind his newspaper when Manjeet came out to the balcony. Seeing Rahul like that, Manjeet chuckled at him. "What's up, bro? How come you are unwinding on the balcony today? This newspaper seems to be just a pretence for doing something else. It seems you've found the USP of our hostel pretty soon, huh?"

"Oh no, Manjeet. It's nothing like that," Rahul winced, suddenly realising the slight impropriety in his behaviour.

"I'm just joking, man. You may continue being your geek self," Manjeet said with a wink. Manjeet was a six-feet-tall young man from Haryana. He had come to Delhi to prepare for competitive examinations and the one for the post of sub inspector. A state-level volleyball player and a fitness freak, he had a well-sculpted face with a slightly pointed chin, broad shoulders and dark curly hair.

The next moment, he elbowed Rahul to have a look at the girl who had just come out on the balcony. "I haven't seen her before. She seems to be new here," said Manjeet, while, at the same time, anxiously hoping to catch a glimpse of Gurleen.

Rahul stole a look at the new girl and was immediately mesmerised. The dark eyes set on a beautiful round face seemed familiar to him. She was squinting as the sun was shining a little too brightly. She slightly flicked her ochre brown hair spiralling down her shoulders. A classic Indian beauty, she oozed sophistication. Rahul involuntarily kept staring at her.

"But wait..." In a flash, Rahul recognised her as Dr Aditi who had helped him in getting Uncle ji treated at the hospital. Rahul wanted to wave at her but did not have the courage to do so. A shy, simple guy from a village, he did not have the guts to make a move at a girl. The moment he recognised Dr Aditi, he started getting butterflies in his stomach. He was observing every move of hers; from her crimson silk jacket to her indigo blue wrap-around skirt with elephant motifs, from her kohl-rimmed eyes to her alluring long curly hair, Rahul found himself smitten by Dr Aditi's beauty. He already had a great admiration for her because of the way she had helped him in getting immediate medical attention for Uncle ji a few months back.

Sensing prying eyes on herself, she shifted her gaze to glance across the balcony at Rahul and Manjeet. She looked at them with a questioning look on her face. Rahul did not realise that he had been staring at Aditi. Also, he didn't expect her to look at him directly. Taken aback by her temerity, Rahul averted his gaze and felt miserable at having projected himself as a voyeur. His heart was beating really fast. He felt embarrassed at his own conduct. It was mortifying to be caught ogling at someone like that. He did not have the audacity to look at her again. Thinking of himself as an idiot, Rahul immediately went inside. Manjeet didn't know what had suddenly come over Rahul. Once inside, he chortled at Rahul, "Why did you come inside so abruptly? You are sweating like a pig. Your cheeks have reddened as if you have put on loads of makeup." Rahul looked at Manjeet and told him about Dr Aditi, whom he had met on his first day in Delhi. He was ashamed of himself for staring at her like a roadside Romeo. Pinching Rahul, Manjeet chuckled, "Good going, bro! You have acclimatised yourself to Delhi pretty soon. I believed myself to be the Romeo of Goyal House but it seems you've even surpassed me. Got to know the best girl, hunn..." Rahul recoiled at such a description, and told Manjeet that he was just misinterpreting the entire thing.

Though what happened was abrupt and quick, Aditi still recognised Rahul as the same boy she had met in the hospital. She caught him gazing at her before he averted his eyes. Her heart skipped a beat too. You do not find such raw, brawny, handsome boys with a certain humbleness in their bearing, in the cities anymore.

Rahul had indeed, been generously blessed by God in the department of looks. Years of physical toil in his village had given him a truly breath-taking, impressive physique. He was wearing a pair of black sweatpants and a sea-blue jacket over a white T-shirt, complementing his physique and toned abs. His muscular body and sculpted looks could give tough competition to anyone and made him look almost like a Greek god. No wonder Aditi could not help but take a second look at him.

In the evening, Rahul again came out on the balcony. Arun and Manjeet were already there. Manjeet, always in a mood to yank someone's chain, told Arun about the morning episode. Arun laughed. "Manjeet, I can believe the sun rises in the west if you say so but not what you are saying about Rahul. You don't know him as I do. He is a saint, man," Arun continued. "But Rahul, if that's true I would be happy for you. Thank God you're finally coming around." Arun winked at Rahul. Just then, Manjeet poked Rahul and asked him to look down at the road. Gurleen and Simran appeared; ready to play badminton at the park. They looked ready to smash the badminton court with their racquets and killer looks. Manjeet asked them if they wanted to go to the park for a walk. Arun already had plans of meeting Anjali at the cafe around the park. He agreed to join them after his assignation.

"You go yourself, Manjeet, otherwise God knows what wild stories you'll make up about me." Rahul got back at Manjeet at the first opportunity.

"Oh, come on, you know what I mean. Nobody takes me seriously here." Manjeet put his arm around Rahul's shoulder and took him along. So Rahul and Manjeet went to the park with their badminton racquets. As they reached the court, they noticed that Anjali and Arun were going towards the cafe.

Gurleen and Simran were already playing badminton when Manjeet approached and asked them if they could play mixed doubles as no other badminton court was free. The girls were hesitant but they agreed. Manjeet had a no-holds-barred attitude and it did not take him long to get into talking terms with Gurleen, the Chandigarh girl, who liked this unabashed Manjeet instantly. They were clearly drawn towards each other.

Rahul sat there watching them playing. Manjeet gelled with them in no time and it was quite a sight to see him playing with the girls. Manjeet was playing opposite Gurleen, with Simran as his partner. There was another girl playing with them. Resting his chin in his hand, he was soon lost in his thoughts. He thought of the day when he saw that doe-eyed doctor in the hospital emerging out of her room like the moon appearing out of the clouds. Her Lakhnavi kurta fell beautifully on her tall and toned body. She had tied her hair in a low bun, exposing her long white neck. Rahul remembered everything, all the details about her. And, when he was speaking to her, he was smitten by her kohl-rimmed eyes below her arched brows.

At night, Rahul couldn't sleep. He could still see Aditi laughing and chatting with her friends. Rahul could not imagine in his wildest dreams that he would get to see that vision of beauty again. In a big city, you meet people and then they get lost in the crowd forever. Rahul had never thought of meeting Aditi again. But to his luck, there she was, staying right across! He could still see her silver hoops dancing in her side-swept hair as she was talking excitedly with Gurleen. Her kohled eyes were gleaming. No, she was not just any woman, pretty to look at. There was something more about her. She was truly beautiful but there was also an air of amazing determination about her. There was no frivolity in her beauty. Her charm was even more, because the strength of her character was apparent in her bearing. Lost in her thoughts he fell asleep.

****

The next day was a Sunday. Rahul woke up pretty early and got ready. He didn't want to miss any opportunity of stealing a glance at Aditi. He had his breakfast and came out on the balcony with his cup of ginger elaichi tea. Manjeet and Arun also joined him on the balcony. Rahul was anxiously looking across as if waiting for somebody. Manjeet sensed his anxiousness and told him that Dr Aditi was visiting her friends and had left. Rahul was taken aback by Manjeet's forthrightness and stammered, "Oh come on man! I was just observing that sparrows are so few around here."

"Stop, Manjeet. He's just indulging in some birdwatching," Arun jeered.

"You both are rascals," Rahul jumped towards the two as both ran inside in a bid to save themselves.

Apart from this light-hearted banter, the day became pretty dull for Rahul. In his heart of hearts, he was dying to get one more glimpse of Aditi. As that hope was lost for the day, nothing interested him anymore. A lovelorn Rahul languished in a corner with a book in his hands for the whole day. Amma had been worried about his safety when Rahul was leaving for Delhi. She asked him to chant Hanuman Chalisa daily lest someone cast any spell on him. Rahul felt that the spell was indeed cast upon him. No amount of praying could protect him now.

****

Rahul was happy with the way his life was going. He was consistently trying to find opportunities to hone his skills. Now he was more accustomed to city life and social behaviour, therein. He believed in working hard and crafting his own destiny. Arun had taught him to ride a bike. Leaving things to sheer fortuitousness was loathsome and a sign of weak men. So far, everything was going well in his life. He was loving this new world filled with a lot of opportunities, positivity and zeal.

Rahul was earning well and his life had certainly turned for the better as compared to his earlier village life. But he missed his family.

One day he called home. A smile appeared on Rahul's face as he heard Baba's voice. Rahul wished him, "Pranam, Baba. How are you?"

Baba spoke with pride and happiness in his voice, "We are fine here, Beta. How are you doing? It's a new city, a new place for you. I know it takes time to adjust to new places. Have you settled yet?"

Rahul sighed and said, "Baba, it is very tough to like a new place so soon. Sometimes I feel very low here. I miss you all. If only you all were here with me it would be so much better." Rahul was highly ambitious but at the core of his heart, he yearned for the life that he led all these years soaking in the warmth and love of his family.

"For sure, I am trying to carve a place for myself here. Balvinder ji, my boss, is a hard taskmaster but at the same time a very decent human being."

Baba comforted him, "You are sincere and hard-working, Beta. Don't worry. Just do your work with honesty. And remember, don't look at the buttered bread of others. 'Big castles are made from small pebbles.' So always collect what you have and utilise it to get better. You can never go wrong with honesty and dedication. Success will come on its own."

"Mm-hmm." Rahul sounded a little blasé, thinking how naive his Baba was about the ways of the world but then added that he would always keep his teachings in mind. He asked Baba whether the salary amount was transferred into Reema Didi's account. Baba replied in the affirmative. Asking to pay regards to Amma, he hung up.

Rahul was working awfully hard and had won the trust of his boss. Rahul would deposit a good percentage of his salary to Reema's account every month so that she could withdraw the money as per their requirements at home. Rahul was enjoying this new phase of his life. He was adapting himself to city life and had even made a few good friends here. Things were looking up for him.

****

Aditi was back at the hospital. Another unnerving day was waiting for her. The OPD was filled with patients jostling to get a seat in the waiting area. Even though summer had not come yet, Aditi was sweating all over. The white coat over her green kurta was making her uncomfortable. The stale air of the OPD was filled with the distinct smell of phenyl. She would often feel like a caged bird there. But today, she felt a strange sensation within her. She could still feel that glance over her body. When she visited Gurleen this time, she had no inkling that she would find that same tall and dashing young man whom she encountered some time ago in the emergency ward. It was a coincidence to find him again; but a happy one at that. Of all the people moving along, this young man had left an indelible impression upon her heart. As she sat in the doctor's duty room, sipping a cup of tea, she thought about him again and again in a way that she had never thought about anyone else. Until she was roused from her meditations when Dr Nikunj entered and addressed her,

"Hey Aditi, what's up? You look lost. Missing me?" he said teasingly and then chortled at his own joshing remark.

Aditi blushed as if her innermost concealed feelings were suddenly exposed. Her cheeks were flushed. But she quickly recovered herself.

"Oh come on, Dr Nikunj. You always tease me like that. I was just thinking about a curious case that came up in the OPD today." She tried to divert the conversation.

"Really? Who blushes like that while thinking about a case in the OPD?" Dr Nikunj quipped.

"Oh wait, it must be a case of some lovelorn guy who has fallen hopelessly in love with a beautiful doctor," Dr Nikunj grinned.

Aditi was losing her cool at Dr Nikunj's banter. She rolled her eyes and feigned anger at him.

"You will never mend your ways. Now get going."

Dr Nikunj chuckled and left the room leaving Aditi fuming. Dr Nikunj had this habit of engaging in such playful banter with Aditi. For Aditi, there was nothing unusual about it. But today, Dr Nikunj's playful banter did one thing. It made her realise that Rahul's effect on her was growing to the extent that now it was also visible to others. Even Dr Nikunj could read the signs of love on her face so clearly. Love had indeed come knocking at her doors. Love strikes like a lightning bolt, so powerful and intense that it can't be denied.

❑

4

CHAPTER

The Looming Crisis

I do not think the forest would be so bright, nor the water so warm, nor love so sweet, if there were no danger in the lakes.

—C S Lewis

Winters had finally paved the way for the king of seasons—Spring. Nature was at its splendid best. The chill in the air had been replaced by a cool breeze. Rahul could feel a lightness in his spirit, a sprint in his feet and a joy in his heart. Holi was just around the corner and Rahul was seeing the city in a different light. Was it the effect of Dr Aditi's proximity, his success in the office or just the colours of the season? He didn't want to think about it. He saw kids pestering passersby with balloons and water gun showers. It was Rahul's first Holi away from his family. Even as he was sad about being away from them, he was excited about all the planning going on in the hostel. Ravi had brought white T-shirts with 'Holi beasts' printed across the chest, for all of them. A grand feast had been planned on their balcony. The halwai had been asked to supply chhole bhature, samose and pakode with *gujiya* and *laddoos*. There had been a big argument over *bhaang* a few days before that. Rahul and Arun were completely against any intoxicant being a part of the celebration. Manjeet's insistence on it being God's prasad didn't prevail with them. All of them agreed on celebrating Holi in an eco-friendly and decent way. Synthetic and artificial colours were completely out of the picture and so was *bhaang*.

No one was aware of the lurking danger. But gradually, the TV and the newspapers were increasingly reporting the havoc that the novel coronavirus was wreaking across the world. A few days before Holi, there was news of people spreading the infection while they themselves were unaware of being infected. A man had thrown a lavish birthday party for his son and had ended up infecting all the families that attended the party. A Bollywood singer attended a pre-Holi bash and all the people who came in contact with her were quarantined after she tested COVID-positive. There was intense contact tracing of people who returned from abroad and were infected. However, these were sporadic incidents of coronavirus infection in the country. Nobody took it very seriously. Nobody believed that they were at risk, and especially the Indians were very boastful of their immunity.

Though a little reticent at first, the Goyal House boys ultimately celebrated Holi with full gusto. Manjeet had even been courageous enough to invite Anjali, Gurleen and Aditi to their hostel in the spirit of festivity. The girls had gracefully accepted the invitation. Rahul was secretly thrilled at the thought of having Dr Aditi over. He knew Manjeet and Gurleen had feelings for each other. Anjali and Arun were already a couple.

The day began with a burst of energy. The group was making merry and smearing each other with colours. They were having a blast. Affection between Arun and Anjali was evident as they couldn't take their eyes off each other even while mingling with the group. Manjeet was the life of the party that day. There was not a single person who was not swayed by his wild and ebullient spirits. Gurleen, the quintessential Punjabi girl, loved this side of Manjeet as she herself was bold as brass. Their conviviality was infectious. Everyone was enjoying the festivities.

Standing beside the large table on which all the snacks were laid was Rahul. He was looking at the party delightedly. Since he was new to this kind of celebration, he felt a little diffident in becoming a part of it all the way. Back in his village, grown-up boys and girls did not play Holi together. Consequently, he had a bit of a culture shock.

The group was dancing to the music by now. But his eyes were fixed on Aditi who was talking excitedly with the girls in a corner. Her white kurta had blue, green and red colours splashed all over. She was his rainbow that appears after the heavy rains. Deep inside, he wished that he had been the one to smear one of those colours on her kurta. When Manish pulled at his hand, he recovered from the reverie. He was being dragged to join the dancing group.

Rahul felt ashamed of his own salacious thoughts. All through the festivities, he was struggling with himself. First the culture shock and then the way Aditi had made him weak in the knees. The tired group finally sat down to gorge on chhole bhature. Just as Rahul settled down with a plate in his hands, he saw Aditi walk towards him with her plate. She sat by his side and addressed him in a nonchalant way.

"So you live here," Aditi spoke as she ate a big bite from her plate.

"Oh yes, Dr Aditi." Rahul had to force the words out of his mouth so unprepared was he for this.

"You can just call me Aditi. What do you do here? You told me in the hospital that you had come from the village. Right?" Aditi continued being upbeat.

"Yes... yes. I've got a job here now." Rahul had recovered himself by now and was quite happy sitting next to the girl he had secretly fallen in love with. He told her all about his new work and his plans for the future. Aditi listened to him absorbedly. As he looked at her face and got lost in the beauty of it, he would forget everything he was saying and start fumbling for words.

"Let's go out on the balcony." She took Rahul's hand and they quickly moved out to the balcony.

Both were standing there. Rahul was still not able to get over the touch of Aditi's hand.

There was too much going on for his heart to process. She was right beside him and talking to him, while he stood there like a fool trying to catching his breath. It took him a while to compose himself.

"You know, I always wanted to get a feel of how it all looks from here." Aditi muttered.

"But why?" Rahul smiled at this silliness of Aditi.

"When all the boys stand here and stare at the girls over there unendingly, I just wonder what feels so amazing to them." Aditi pointed towards Tulip hostel. Rahul felt embarrassed at being exposed.

"But hey, it's pretty boring. Isn't it?"

Rahul smiled and said, "No, you won't understand because what boys stare at is not an empty balcony."

Both laughed.

****

Though Rahul was annoyed at his initial awkward behaviour with Aditi, yet he revelled in the memories of the little chit-chat that he had with her.

While Rahul was revelling in these little inconsequential encounters with the secret love of his life, there was a danger lurking around. The Wuhan virus was spreading across the world and was soon expected to raise its ugly head closer home.

The buzz had started. It became a hot topic of discussion everywhere. After dinner, all the boys gathered around on the roof and started discussing how a tiny bat virus had ravaged the world.

Wuhan virus.

What's that?

Ankur, who was preparing for the Civil Services Exam, found the perfect opportunity to exhibit his knowledge and so began expounding, "It spreads due to bats. Bats are eaten by people in some countries like Vietnam, Thailand, China and Indonesia. Bats are consumed on a large scale in these places. This new virus has made a jump from bats to humans." Ankur surely must have made his notes on coronavirus lest the topic comes up in the examination.

Manish, who loved reading crime thrillers, had another opinion on this. "It's a man-made virus and will be used as a biological weapon. It is a new kind of warfare among the countries of the world. Scientists from big and developed countries invent new bacteria and viruses to create havoc in the world."

Some, like Ravi, analysed the situation in a more philosophical light. He sermonised, "Life is so unpredictable and this new virus has proved it again. No matter what man thinks, God has his own ways. That is why the virus has spread across continents within a matter of a few days."

Rahul was listening to them all and on his turn adopted a more worldly stance. "It looks like someone from outside comes and what we have imagined to be indestructible so far falls down like a house of cards. This miniscule virus is a blow to our complacency".

Arun, who was a dab hand at world news, was quick to explore the issue from a different perspective. He opined, "The European continent has suffered a lot and now the day is not far when this devil will take India in its grip. The so-called developed countries of Europe and the USA have struggled to contain this virus as no medicine is proving to be effective against it. The virus has brought the mightiest of countries to their knees."

"Healthcare infrastructures are collapsing in various developed countries even where the population is less as this virus is spreading unabated." Ashok, another hosteller, was quick to add.

All the boys had different perspectives on the Wuhan virus. The virus had created a ripple in their otherwise drab existence. Those who were of a more sceptical disposition blamed it on China. The ones with a devout character called it a turn of fate. But the one thing that they all agreed to was that it presented a mortal danger for the country.

Far away from the drawing-room discussions, the Wuhan virus had taken the world by storm. It was on a killing spree. And the most disturbing fact was that the contagion was spreading at an astronomical rate. The smiles on the faces of people had turned into despair and fear. Initially, no one had thought how dangerous this virus would turn out to be but the repercussions were alarming and egregious.

The obvious question in everyone's mind was:

What will happen if it comes to India?

Reports on the deadly virus had been doing rounds since December, but the danger is not real until it knocks at your doors. There was a palpable fear among people as the peril was imminent now.

The next day, in the office too, people discussed about the novel coronavirus. Words like novel, virus, pandemic, COVID, etc. were catching up on the day-to-day vocabulary of people. Advices abound whenever any new incident strikes. Everyone had a word or two of advice to offer in the office.

Balvinder Singh said, "The government should take strict measures, otherwise no one would survive. We are the second largest populated country in the world. We cannot withstand an onslaught like that."

Arun agreed. "Our medical facilities and healthcare infrastructure are insufficient. This virus has already smashed the pride of so-called developed countries."

The cases in India were very few till the first week of March 2020. Nobody felt it to be a cause of concern until it started flashing on their TV screens in a big way. Not even when the health minister of the country had to come ahead and assure that the government of India was constantly monitoring the situation and was taking all the necessary steps to avoid the spread of the virus.

But it was a ticking bomb all along.

Soon, social media was flooded with perturbing videos of people undergoing the ordeal in other countries. The spectacle of death was looming large. Visuals of the sufferings of people were spreading terror across the world. Increasing numbers of deaths were being reported across the globe.

On 14 March 2020, Balvinder Singh received a call from Inderjeet Singh, his brother-in-law, who was in Venice with his family. He was petrified and cried for help. Balvinder Singh consoled him and assured him, "Things will turn out fine. Have patience."

Inderjeet narrated the horrific situation in Venice. He told Balvinder, "The virus will not spare anyone. People are dying here; I have lost many of my friends. We are not safe here. God knows what will happen. The medical infrastructure has collapsed. Even doctors are dying here. We are living in our houses like prisoners and there is lockdown. No one is allowed to go outside. Take care of yourselves." The call got disconnected abruptly.

Balvinder Singh was horror-struck. He called Arun and Rahul and told them about the call and his brother-in-law's sufferings in Venice. Rahul tried to console him, but Balvinder Singh was in no mood for a conversation anymore and said, "I am not feeling well and am leaving for home. Take care of the office."

In the evening, Rahul and Arun discussed the situation at length. Both felt bad for Balvinder Singh. But there was nothing that anyone could do. Suddenly, the mobile phone rang; Arun heard Anjali's voice on the other side. She was frightened and sobbing.

Arun was numb. "What happened? Why are you crying?

"Corona has swallowed Naresh Mama's family. They are in France. Two years ago, he was deputed to France for a term of three years. He had been living there with his family. For the last ten days, no one from the family was picking our calls. We tried our best to contact him but our efforts went in vain. Just an hour earlier, Jatin Mama received a call from Paris. A policeman told him that Naresh Mama's entire family had succumbed to the virus." She cried inconsolably while saying these words.

Arun tried to console her. "Anjali, don't cry. I am with you. I am coming." And he left to meet Anjali during this difficult time.

Such tales of suffering were floating around. The horror was real and near.

Rahul thought to himself, "Although cases are less in our country, we should follow norms as per the direction of our government, otherwise, we may have to face a more critical state of affairs than Europe. This is an alarming situation."

What steps would India take? This question worried everyone.

At dinner time, all the hostel boys were hooked on the news channel. The news flashed on the screen reporting an increase in the number of cases. The situation was finally taking a turn for the worse.

Ankur said, "Oh God! Now this devil has started spreading its wings here too."

Arun decided to adopt a cautious approach and called Avtaar ji, the hostel guard. He instructed, "Avtaar ji, do not allow anyone without wearing a mask in the hostel building."

Rahul concurred. "Avtaar ji, the situation has become serious. We should get hands sanitised of every person visiting our hostel. We will arrange for the sanitisers by tomorrow."

****

It was 20 March 2020. Rahul and his friends were watching the news on TV when a headline suddenly flashed on the screen declaring that the prime minister would address the nation at 8 p.m.

In the evening, everyone was glued to the screen to see what the honourable PM was going to say. There was a shroud of silence in the room as everyone listened with bated breath.

In his address to the nation, the PM asked all to be alert. The complacency on the part of people was somewhat responsible for the sudden spurt of the virus-borne disease in various countries. The PM assured people that the government machinery was keeping a close vigil on the situation. Isolation seemed to be the only remedy in sight to break the chain, witnessing the extensive impact of COVID-19 in developed countries. He announced a 'Janta curfew' to be observed on Sunday 22 March from 7:00 a.m. to 9:00 p.m. and appealed to everyone saying no citizen, barring those engaged in essential services, should get out of home.

'Janta curfew' was an act of self-isolation by people. It was aimed at breaking the chain of spread of the virus.

The PM also urged the nation to applaud at 5 p.m. the selfless work of essential services personnel. The PM said the government will constitute a COVID-19 task force to handle the economic challenges arising from the spread of virus and the resultant impact on various sectors of economy. He stressed the need to avoid panic buying and assured that the government was taking all steps to ensure that supply of essential commodities was not disrupted.

Advisories and guidelines were being issued by the government. People were asked not to visit hospitals for routine checkups and postpone surgeries, if not mandatory. There was also an appeal to business committees and enterprises to act humanely and not cut the wages of their employees in these dire circumstances.

Arun and the other hostel boys were quite enthusiastic about the janta curfew.

Arun said, “The PM has given a call for the nation. Ankur, remember how we used to run those campaigns in college?”

Ankur chipped in. “And those nukkad nataks too. Remember how successful was the one that we staged in the university grounds during the anti-corruption campaign?”

Rahul said, “Sounds interesting. Let’s have another like it; an awareness campaign for this pandemic.”

Arun agreed, “Hmm... why not? I’m in.”

Rahul and Arun were raring to do something in those extraordinary circumstances. All of them decided to run an awareness campaign. The Tulip hostel girls too helped them in designing banners and making arrangements. This was an opportunity for Manjeet and Gurleen to spend time together. They looked into each other’s eyes and smiled. Rahul was missing Aditi. Gurleen could sense this and nudged Manjeet.

In the morning, the boys reached the nearby park and then left in small groups for the scheduled places with microphones and banners.

They were carrying colourful posters with salutary messages for the corona warriors. Arun and Rahul directed the whole team and everything went as planned. The vigour with which they ran the campaign did create a stir in the neighbourhood and made people aware of the necessity of isolating themselves to break the chain.

Arun and Rahul had become popular in their neighbourhood. They were the torchbearers, the natural leaders. Aditi heard about this campaign from Gurleen. She had one more reason to be impressed with the already irresistible Rahul.

Two days passed and 22 March came with Janta Curfew. The whole area wore a deserted look. Roads were empty. Vehicles carrying essential commodities were plying on the roads. People were inside their houses watching television and discussing the next step of the government.

****

It was not easy to accept this sudden change in the manner that people were used to living their lives. Everyone was dismayed at this onslaught of the pandemic. A generation that lived at jet speed had to abruptly pull its reins. The fast pace of life was brought to a halt as if someone had hit the brakes suddenly.

Rahul was sauntering on the roof. He was wondering about Dr Aditi. This was what he used to do whenever he would be alone. What must be going on with her? After all, she was a doctor and was in the most precarious of situations. He was deeply concerned for her. If only he could be with her, and protect her from anything and everything. Rahul was restless. It had been a while since he saw her last.

Just then, he saw Gurleen on the roof of her hostel, across the street, talking to someone over the phone. Rahul could not control himself. He waved at her and when she looked towards him, he enquired about Dr Aditi. Gurleen told him that Aditi was at the hospital and the workload had greatly increased for doctors. When Rahul asked if Dr Aditi was fine, Gurleen assured him that she was doing well.

What Rahul did not know was that it was indeed Aditi with whom Gurleen was talking to over the phone. Aditi asked Gurleen who this person was enquiring about her.

Gurleen told her that it was the new boy, Rahul, and how he surprisingly was very concerned about Aditi. Aditi blushed. This feeling that someone cared for her deeply stirred the emotions of love in her. She was falling hopelessly in love with Rahul.

The brewing love and attraction between Rahul and Aditi did not fail to reveal itself to Gurleen, who was happy for them. She called out to Rahul and said,

"Hey, Rahul! You know Dr Aditi would be very happy if you ask her directly."

Rahul was not prepared for this outrightness on Gurleen's part. He was too hesitant to say anything.

Gurleen was unstoppable. She further said in a teasing manner, "98743...is her number, dude," and guffawed. Aditi was still on the line. She was embarrassed at Gurleen's childlike and blunt behaviour. Aditi feigned anger and disconnected the call.

After about a minute or so, Aditi saw a notification on her phone screen. There was a message from an unknown number. Aditi's heart was racing as she opened the message box. It was a short message—

Hi Dr Aditi, hope you are fine. I was just concerned about you. The view from our balcony doesn't look so good anymore.

Take care. Rahul

Aditi felt a tidal wave of emotions at this moment. The remark about the balcony made her break out into a wide smile. There was so much that she wanted to write, but stopped short for fear of seeming too desperate. Still, she could not stop herself from responding in return.

"Yeah, I'm fine. Thanks for the concern".

While on the one hand a new chapter had begun in the lives of Rahul and Aditi with these messages, on the other hand the country was gearing itself up for the grave danger that had knocked at its doors. Love was beginning to bloom in turbulent times indeed.

❑

5

CHAPTER

Lockdown

Home is a shelter for storms—all sorts of storms.

—William J Bennett

23 March 2020

Rahul and Arun were back from the office.

There was quite a bit of speculation since the media reported during the day that the prime minister would address the nation again at 8 p.m. Everyone was busy finishing the tasks for the day in anticipation of it. All the boys gathered in the common room after dinner and were anxiously waiting for the clock to strike 8. The tense atmosphere was weighing heavily on everyone. They were avoiding each other's gaze and hoping against all odds that the prime minister's address would bring them some relief.

The PM went on from thanking the people for making janta curfew a success to elucidating the need to follow social distancing norms and COVID-appropriate behaviour. From thereon, it became somewhat clear that something unprecedented was going to happen. And the announcement finally came which was a jolt for everyone. A complete nationwide lockdown was announced for a period of 21 days to prevent the spread of infection.

The boys were taken aback at this sudden move. Everyone was silent as if still processing what just flashed on the TV screen. A 21-day complete national lockdown was no mean thing. No wonder— it was the largest of its kind too.

"Whoooo!"

All were dumbfounded by this unforeseen announcement. Rahul and Arun looked at each other in amazement. No one had ever heard of such a situation. It was a bolt out of the blue.

This was followed by quite a spirited discussion among the boys over the situation. Arun, Rahul and Manjeet went to the roof for a walk after dinner. The stars were twinkling in the sky and the moon was playing hide and seek behind the clouds. A soothing breeze was blowing. The usual hustle and bustle of everyday life had disappeared, and everything was wrapped in a shroud of silence. A temperate atmosphere belying the turbulence that had turned up at their doors.

They talked first about the janta curfew and then about the lockdown. Manjeet's eyes fell on Gurleen who was on the roof of her hostel too. Her upright posture made her look taller than her five feet three inches. She wore a white salwar kameez and a fuchsia dupatta with silver piping. Her loose hair blowing with the breeze slightly touched her face every now and then. Manjeet was smitten by the sparkle in her eyes and the warmth in her smile. She waved at Manjeet. Manjeet waved back too. He was no longer listening to the lockdown discussion. His attention was riveted on something else.

"I don't think it's the end, rather it's the beginning of something even bigger."

Arun replied with concern, "Yes, you are right, Rahul. It's high time now to take some strident steps as COVID-19 is a fatal disease and even the developed countries have failed to tackle it."

Rahul added, "India has already crossed the mark of 500 cases by now and they are increasing at a fast rate."

Arun sounded concerned. "The death toll will be really high if it spreads in India the way it has in Europe."

"Remember how Italy has crumbled under it." Rahul noticed as he spoke that Manjeet had drifted away and was busy talking to Gurleen by now.

Arun was really perturbed. "Rahul I'm worried about it now. If it spreads, it's going to be a disaster."

Rahul, who was always the voice of reason in the group, tried to comfort him. "Don't panic, mate. We all are together in this. We will do whatever it takes. If we just follow the protocol, it will be under control."

Rahul continued, "We will encourage all the boys to follow social distancing norms and avoid going outside unnecessarily. And if they have to go out in case of any emergency, then they must wear a mask. We would persuade them to follow COVID-appropriate behaviour till further orders."

****

The next day witnessed the fallout of the announcement of a lockdown.

As the day passed, rumour mills were busy churning out all sorts of misinformation. This had already started creating panic among people. There was no dearth of unscrupulous people as well. Hoarders were trying to cash in on the situation. The kirana shop owners raised the prices of essential items. The medical stores were raising the prices of basic medicines. Fruit and vegetable vendors also followed in their footsteps. People were indulging in panic buying and stocking food grains, vegetables, etc. This got Rahul to contemplate.

The situation seemed fine on the surface, but discontent, doubt and fear were brewing deep under. News channels and social media were abuzz with the rising mortality rates in the affected countries. Black marketing, sky-high prices of essential goods and fear of getting infected from the coronavirus were becoming a cause for people's melancholy. Circumstances in the villages were comparatively under control.

While the political scene was getting all ugly and dismal, the boys in the hostel were bracing themselves to face the challenges coming ahead. Rahul received a call from his sister enquiring about his whereabouts. He assured her of his well-being and asked her to take good care of Amma and Baba.

Till late in the night, the entire hostel was reverberating with the sounds of boys talking to their families and reassuring them of their safety. For the first time, people felt the agony of birds kept in cages. Now they were fluttering inside their houses like their winged friends, unable to go out for fear that they might catch the COVID-19 disease.

Isolation often leads to depression. This isolation that was suddenly forced upon people was not easy to deal with.

****

Barren roads, closed markets and deserted buildings of offices, schools and colleges, greeted Delhi roads. The city bore a desolate look.

The police had imposed section 144 of the CrPC which prohibited assembly of five or more people at one place. The National Disaster Management Act was invoked across the nation. Only the essential services were functioning.

Rahul was taken by surprise when he went out to buy groceries. He could not believe it was the same city that he had embraced only a few months back. When he reached the supermarket, he found that the guard was checking everyone's temperature through a thermal scanner and spraying their hands with sanitiser before giving them entry. They were not allowing entry to more than five people at one time. Others had to wait outside for their turn, maintaining social distancing. It was a relief to see that people were acting responsibly.

Finally as Rahul got entry, he quickly began to look for the things that he had to buy. It was not easy to look for things, drag the cart while maintaining minimal contact with any surface and also ensuring that you did not touch your mask again and again. For all those reasons, Rahul did not have any inkling of who was standing beside him rummaging through the cosmetics section. Only when he moved to cross past her did he recognise that it was none else but Dr Aditi.

Aditi also looked back at him while moving aside to give him passage. Their eyes met and both smiled behind their masks. They spoke simultaneously,

"Hi... you here?"

Aditi leaned forward and motioned to drop the shampoo bottle that she had got hold of after so much of rummaging through the shelves into the cart. But since all her attention was riveted at Rahul, the bottle fell out of the cart rather than in. Rahul saw this and quickly moved to lend a helping hand to Aditi. Aditi was inwardly angry at herself for acting so clumsily in front of Rahul. And thus she smacked her forehead.

"I'm done. Have you bought your things?"

"Yeah... I was just leaving."

"Shall we go for billing then?"

Rahul moved towards the billing counter. Aditi followed behind him.

"Come on, I'll drop you." Rahul offered Aditi a lift on his bike which Aditi accepted gleefully.

Rahul carried both the bags while moving towards the bike despite Aditi's protests. Aditi could not help but steal a glance at Rahul. She wondered how agile he was despite being so robust. And how humble, despite being so handsome. His muscular arms were even more prominent as he carried those two heavy bags.

"How would it feel to be encircled by those strong and muscular arms?" Aditi was lost in such thoughts. She felt herself to be weak and stupid at the same time to harbour such feelings for a boy whom she had known for barely four months. What she was completely ignorant of was that Rahul himself was harbouring equally mushy feelings for her.

As the bike began to cruise on the road, Aditi put her hand on Rahul's shoulder. Rahul had heard from Manjeet how the latter used to speed up the bike and especially more so around a speed breaker so that Gurleen would hold him tighter. There was a speed breaker ahead and so was Rahul's chance to get closer to Aditi, albeit by way of mischief. Rahul increased the speed. But as the bike drew closer to the speed breaker, Rahul slowed down and negotiated the bike gently over it. The bike glided smoothly over the speed breaker and Rahul heaved a sigh of relief that he did not succumb to cheap tactics. But the next moment, he felt her soft arm sliding around his waist and holding him tightly. The trick worked without even being implemented. Rahul was on cloud nine.

Aditi was getting so hopelessly drawn towards Rahul that she could not and did not even see any point in resisting the surge of love within her being.

When she alighted from the bike, Rahul handed the bag to her.

"Here... take care. Don't forget to sanitise them," Rahul said looking into her eyes and smiling from behind his mask.

At this, Aditi bent forward and gave him a polite hug. Rahul was not prepared for this and so did not even realise how to react to this.

Aditi whispered in his ears, "Bye," and turned and walked away.

Rahul's heart was thumping. It took him a moment to compose himself. Long after she left could he utter the word bye in reply. He kick-started the bike and kept repeating the word bye to himself in the same hushed tone that Aditi spoke in.

****

The nature of the office work changed with the onset of lockdown. Balvinder asked Arun and Rahul to work from home and visit the office only when required. Rahul was given a laptop for this. This new work regime was quite enervating as one had to remain glued to the laptop for the whole day. The work life had infringed upon the personal life of people.

Ankur's coaching institute was shut too. The institute was offering online classes to the students. Everyone in Goyal House was thus adapting themselves to the new mores.

The lockdown period saw an increasing use of technology. Everyone—schools, colleges and workplaces—was turning to a digital mode of functioning. Technology became the saving grace for education. Pintu's school too had switched over to online classes for the students. When Rahul called home, Pintu was quick to put forth his demand for a smartphone much to the chagrin of Amma. Rahul asked Amma not to worry about these expenses. He assured Pintu that he would immediately order a smartphone online.

What initially felt like a paradisiacal experience began to feel oppressive with time. People were getting restless, living within the confines of their homes. It was the same feeling in all households. Children had lost their vivacity. For a few days they enjoyed being at home, but missed their cricket, badminton and other games where they laughed and enjoyed themselves with their friends. Children studying in the board classes were worried about their future. Headlines on news channels were scaring the people out of their wits. Orchards had been turned into cemeteries as there was not enough space to bury people. The fear of uncertainty was looming large. What scared everyone the most was that even the healthcare workers such as doctors, nurses, ward boys, police personnel and other official staff were being infected by the coronavirus. Increasing number of deaths was gripping the imagination of people with fear and agony.

Rahul was deeply concerned about Aditi's safety in the hospital. His concern gave him the courage to become more candid with Aditi. He was constantly in touch with her through calls and messages. The hesitancy was giving way to propinquity.

****

5 April 2020

It was a Sunday. A day to show solidarity in the fight against the pandemic and gratitude towards those who were working at the frontlines. People lit diyas, candles and even flashed their phones at 9 p.m.

Goyal House boys did it. And so did Tulip hostel girls. The way candles and diyas were lit everywhere gave the impression as if Diwali had come around.

For Rahul it was Diwali indeed. In the dim and shimmering light of candles on the opposite balcony, he saw the most beautiful face in the world. Aditi smiled at him. He smiled back. A meaningful smile, hiding behind it the ever-growing love for each other.

****

The poor labour class was the worst hit due to the lockdown. It seemed that lack of work and earning would kill them first before infection by the deadly virus. Livelihood of these workers was at risk.

Several hunger relief camps and shelter homes were created to facilitate such people. Many government institutions like schools and colleges were converted into temporary shelters and hunger relief centres. School teachers and other government officials were deployed to serve in these relief centres.

It was upon the shoulders of the District Magistrates and SDMs to carry out the enormous task of setting up these relief centres overnight. Many teams, including the administrative staff, policemen, civil defence volunteers and NGOs worked together to handle this.

Ravi, who visited the hostel accommodation often, had a Master’s in Social Work. He was actively involved with NGOs called Sahyog Care for You and Aasra. Since the lockdown, these NGOs had been involved with food distribution work. For the hostel boys, he was the window to the world that was bearing the direct brunt of the lockdown. He would often narrate the situation to them.

One day he said,

"The government has been running hunger relief centres in most of the schools to help the needy and the poor. Yesterday, I went to a nearby school to check whether the food distribution was being done properly or not. There I saw pregnant ladies, small children as well as old men standing in long queues waiting patiently to get food for their families." Rahul, Arun, Manjeet and others were listening to these tales of agony with heavy hearts.

He added, "It's hard to see people with hunger and tears gleaming in their eyes. They stared everywhere in the hope of getting food. They waited impatiently for their turn. Each step taken forward in the queue made them hopeful that soon they would get food for their families. The teachers, school staff and civil defence volunteers were working selflessly under the supervision of the district administration. An army of newly appointed civil defence volunteers controlled and maintained the norms of social distancing in the queues. They made people realise that food was sufficient, and that they all would be given food. They requested everyone to follow the guidelines. I too helped in controlling the crowd."

Rahul felt a strong pull to contribute to this noble cause of helping people in such dire circumstances as he heard all such stories of survival for existence from Ravi. So he too joined the NGO Sahyog Care for You on Ravi's exhortation. One day, Rahul got a call from Ravi asking for help in maintaining order during a food distribution drive in a nearby slum.

At around 12 noon, they reached the slum in a minibus. As soon as the bus reached there, people gathered all around the bus with their empty utensils and eyes brimming with tears and hunger. Seeing this, Rahul was affected by the pain and misery of those people. The children had lost their sprightliness due to hunger pangs.

Rahul's eyes welled up. He turned his face towards Arun and said, "And I thought I was in pain. Just look at these people. The young kids who should have been playing around without a hint of worry are here crying and queuing up for food. The old who should have been sitting and talking on the porch are standing here with arched backs and anguished eyes. How did we end up like this, brother? It is the sad reality of our society. These labourers who toiled all their lives to erect these mega cities are dying due to starvation. The same city has turned its back on them and left them in the lurch."

When Rahul and his teammates got off the bus, a teammate asked a civil defence volunteer, "Shyam ji, why have you not maintained a proper queue, following social distancing norms?"

Shyam ji replied, "Suresh ji, hunger knows no rules. These people are starving; they are not concerned about the virus. The only thing they want is food. See here, this lady is 7 months pregnant but still standing here since 8 in the morning so that she could arrange food for her other two children. Her husband also has gone to get food from another nearby school. Look at those small kids with large canisters in their hands. Their childhood is weighed down under the burden of hunger. They have been standing here since 7 in the morning. Now you tell me, how can I force them to stand in queues following social distancing norms? Each and every person here has different stories of struggles. Don't get me started on that. It will be too hard to bear, my friend! Too hard to bear!"

Saying this, Shyam ji went ahead and busied himself in exhorting people to make proper lines. Rahul was instructing volunteers about the modalities of food distribution and everything was running smoothly. But Rahul was uneasy by what Shyam ji had said, and so he went ahead and started a conversation with Shyam ji, enquiring more about the problems faced by people there.

Shyam ji replied, "Sir, there is no end to the problems of these people. Most of them have left their villages and families behind and come here in search of work. But after the lockdown, no one is left with any work. They are daily wagers; they don't have much savings. They have a hand to mouth existence. They have to pay rent for the rooms they live in, and without any work they are in danger of losing those also. They constructed the whole city with their bare hands but could not raise a house for themselves. Look, they are dying of hunger. They want to go back to their villages, their families, but there is no way out to be seen."

Shyam ji added, "I myself have gone through it all. I live nearby and lost my job too. Times were difficult. But then, some friends told me about getting duties as a civil defence volunteer as I had earlier received the basic training. I got this job by the grace of God, through the district administration."

After the food distribution, Rahul went to the slums with Shyam ji and tried to reach out to people and know about their problems. He met a worker Nathu Lal who narrated his story thus, “Brother, I am the only child of my parents and have a wife and three children in the family. My parents had a small piece of land where we used to grow wheat but after a flood in our village, we had nothing to eat. It was then that I migrated here in search of a livelihood in 2017. I earn daily wages and whatever little I save, I send it to my family. Now, I do not have any work. How will I feed my family?” His voice trembled and he started crying while saying this. Rahul tried to console him, but failed. Thousands of such stories were there waiting to be told. If only they could find a patient ear and a compassionate heart.

Rahul was moved by the sad spectacle around him. He felt completely helpless. His thoughts turned to his own family at home. How would they be fighting this pandemic without him being there? He thought about his own mother who always told him everything was fine there each time he called them as they were using the cash which they had saved for his elder sister. Was she really telling the truth, or was she trying to hide their situation from him? He yearned to run back to his family at that instant. But the sobs of people around stopped him. He wanted to do something for them. He assured Nathu Lal that he would find a way to help him. As he met a lot of people from slums, he realised most of them desired to go back to their villages.

When he reached the NGO after distributing food, he talked to the NGO head, Mr Dayal about the whole situation. Dayal Babu was also very concerned about this.

He replied, “Give me some time. I will talk to the SDM of this area, Dr Ehsan. He is very actively involved in all the work. He will surely do something.” He eulogised the area SDM and his works.

❑

6

CHAPTER

Migrants, Miseries and Displacement

No one leaves home unless home is
the mouth of a shark.

—***Warsan Shire***

Rahul found himself in the midst of a world that was collapsing around him. He was in a city that had harboured and sustained thousands like him migrating to its shores in search of a better life and livelihood. But the lockdown was a period of great flux. It laid bare the bitter truth of the transience of human life on the one hand and the deep divide existing in the society on the other. The major brunt of the lockdown was borne by the labourers and the migrant workers who had no means of sustaining themselves after having gone jobless.

When the axe of lockdown fell upon the livelihood of the labourers and daily wagers, they were uprooted instantaneously. It was a death blow for them. Who could understand the pain of these uprooted people better than the one who himself had left his shore in search of better avenues just a few months ago! Rahul was moved by what unfolded in the coming days, but he did not remain a mute spectator to this. He did all that was there in his power and more, staying true to his benevolent nature.

Life had indeed been a roller coaster ride for him in the past months. Everything came in his life simultaneously; his job, the city of his dreams and his lady love. And as if it was not already enough, a virus came sweeping along leaving destruction in its wake.

Rahul was sitting in his room. He was texting Aditi. They texted each other throughout the day, telling each other every little detail of their day. Rahul's day did not start without looking at his phone in the hope that there would be a message from Aditi. Rahul would often think that he had become addicted to messaging. Aditi too would become restless if she did not get any message from Rahul every hour or so. Initially, the messages were sporadic and circumspect. But as their friendship blossomed further and they became more comfortable in writing to each other, the messages became more frequent and more endearing in tone.

Before long they became connected on social media too. Rahul would keep checking her profile pictures, swooning over her mesmerising beauty. Aditi's beauty shone through her simplicity. Pouting faces and camera filters were not her things. She was pretty in her own being. The kind of beauty that is becoming quite rare in the times of beauty filters whereby one cannot make out real from fake. Perhaps, this was also the reason that Rahul, a simple-hearted person himself, was drawn towards her.

'Hey, miss you!' Just when Rahul hit the send button with these words to Aditi, Manjeet peeped into his room and asked him to hurry and see the news flashing on TV.

Rahul came out and got on the sofa. The news channels were flooded with the reports of thousands of people being stranded at the inter-state bus terminus of Anand Vihar. Many rumours were doing the rounds, and one was that inter-state bus services had resumed. This led people to throng to the bus terminus in large numbers in the hope of getting on a bus to their native lands. News channels were frantically covering the whole incident emphasising the threat that a large gathering of this kind posed to everyone. If infection spreads from even one person, it would become impossible to control and track the infected people and break the chain.

People had lost their jobs and one could not survive in cities without having money. Rahul was restless and was tapping his feet on the floor. His anger was trying to find words.

"Where are those politicians now? When election time comes, they are all over the place. But now, when a catastrophe of this degree has struck, they are all talk and no cider," Rahul was seething.

Hearing of politicians and their politics, Manjeet and Arun got into a debate over political parties. Rahul was in no mood to get into this. His heart went out to those who were left in the lurch by this pandemic.

In no time, Rahul received a call from Dayal Babu, the NGO head, who asked him to go to the bus terminus and distribute food to people stranded there. Rahul's restless spirits seized the opportunity and he quickly left.

When Rahul reached there, he was sweating all over. Even though the notoriously hot month of June was quite far away, it was muggy enough to break anyone's spirits. Scores of people were stranded there. The scenario was such that it was difficult to find space on the ground to even set a foot. There were hordes of people everywhere with sacks and bags in their hands and on their heads. Some carried kids on their shoulders, all in the hope of finding a way back to their homes in far-flung areas. The police force had swung into action and made people stand in queues. The long serpentine queues did not seem to end as more and more people flowed into them.

Rahul heard someone saying, "Forget corona, we would die of hunger if we lived here, and then who would perform our last rites? I do not have anyone here. My whole family is in the village. Let alone last rites, they would not even get to know that I am no more. If death is the end, then I want to die in my home with my family by my side."

As the situation had gone out of control, the administration planned to provide buses for the migrants. But this was a humongous task at such short notice.

Rahul was distributing food packets when he heard Dr Ehsan's name. He turned back and saw someone talking to Dr Ehsan about the situation at a little distance from him. It was the same Dr Ehsan of whom Dayal Babu was talking very highly. Rahul's interest was roused. His eyes were now fixed on that commanding figure. Though the situation was a tough one to deal with, Dr Ehsan was at it with all his heart. He was constantly moving around checking everything personally. He had a team of people dealing with it all with sedulous care.

For the last four days, Dr Ehsan had barely managed to sleep for more than a couple of hours. Such was the condition in the capital city.

Rahul reached out to Dr Ehsan. He offered, “Sir, I am Rahul and I work with an NGO called Sahyog. It would be an honour if I could be of any use. Is there anything which I can help with?”

Dr Ehsan was pleased to see such drive. He smiled and said, “Yes, sure, young man. The administrative team is trying its best to provide every service they can, but you see that restlessness is increasing amongst the people. Many of them have started for their homes on foot, out of desperation. If you really want to do something, then try to persuade these people and convince them that we are making arrangements for them soon. Dissuade them from undertaking these perilous journeys.”

What Rahul witnessed there, that day, was a large exodus of people. He was witnessing the migrant workers who came to cities in search of work and livelihood, and were migrating back with feelings of rejection and betrayal at the hands of an antagonistic city. The sight was poignant. Rahul ran around imploring the people not to panic.

It was only after an enormous amount of effort on everybody’s part that they succeeded in convincing the workers and labourers to not pay heed to the rumours. With much persuasion, they succeeded in convincing them to go to their places or shelter homes till the train and bus services were resumed.

This unabating enthusiasm of Rahul did not fail to make an impression on Dr Ehsan. He walked up to Rahul and appreciated his efforts. He allowed Rahul to set up the free food distribution counter.

****

Gurleen's hand was moving deftly as she tossed the boiled rice into the spices with a spatula. The distinct aroma of saffron and other herbs that wafted in the air boosted her confidence in her newly acquired culinary skills. Biryani was Gurleen's project for the day that she undertook for Manjeet. Ever since the lockdown began, she was hooked to Ranveer Brar's cooking channel so much so that one day Manjeet teasingly asked her to cook something for him too. Manjeet had come over to her hostel to savour the feast. While Gurleen was hard at work in the kitchen, Manjeet was watching a new web series on his laptop.

"You can call Rahul and Arun too. I have cooked enough for everyone."

Gurleen spoke loudly from the kitchen.

"I don't think they will come. Arun is doing his office work and Rahul is out on his NGO errands." Manjeet replied, absorbed in the web series. Gurleen could hardly comprehend anything from what came like a mumbling sound and further drowned under the voice of Ranveer Brar playing on her phone.

Lockdown had changed the social scene in many ways. For the affluent and the middle-class people, it came as a period of respite from their otherwise fast-paced and busy lives. They enjoyed this phase as the much-needed break, that they always craved for, to spend time with their loved ones. OTT platforms were witnessing unprecedented subscriptions and cooking channels were receiving millions of hits on their otherwise scarcely visited web pages.

While on one hand Manjeet and Gurleen were gorging on biryani and binge-watching web series, Rahul was in an entirely different world. This world was not geographically removed from the previous one. Rather, there was a deep sociological divide between the two. For the migrant workers and labourers of the city, lockdown came like a disaster that uprooted them instantly and left them hungry and homeless with nowhere to go. Lockdown was a hard blow on them that took away their jobs and homes from them. They did not have the resources to provide meals to their families.

Rahul was returning from the hunger relief centre with a heavy heart. He, along with the others who were engaged at the frontline, was sitting silently in the minibus that ferried them from one centre to another throughout the day. Rahul was brooding over the sufferings of all those afflicted people when the bus jerked to a halt. The driver announced that it would take some time to repair it, and all would have to wait. Rahul climbed down and sat on a concrete block by the side of the road. He was tired. His head was throbbing, and the clamour of woebegone slum dwellers was still ringing in his head.

Just then he saw a bunch of people walking down the road carrying their belongings in bundles. Rahul was not surprised at this. Back in the slum he had seen that many people had resolved to move back to their native places. The city was no longer hospitable to them. Landlords were demanding rent which the daily wagers had no means of paying back. The outcome was disastrous for them; first they went jobless and now homeless.

But what caught Rahul's attention all the more was a woman in the group on whose shoulder a limping man was leaning. The woman, who was walking barefoot, was holding a bundle on her head, and supporting a man on her shoulder. In a bid to help, Rahul ran towards them and asked,

"Where are you all going like this?"

At this, the group pulled up and looked towards him. They were ragged and smeared in dust. "We are from Aligarh. We are going back to our village there," one of them replied.

"Where else would we go?" another muttered in displeasure at the unsolicited inquiry.

Rahul was disconcerted. "How are you going? On foot? It will take you days to reach home!"

"Brother, we are poor, and that is our biggest fault. Look at me, I am a whitewasher, but I lost my work due to the lockdown. How can we survive here without work?" said one of them in a grievous voice.

Rahul was dazed by the misery of these people. The paradox of life was all too visible. People who constructed houses for others and painted them in many colours were themselves left homeless. Their own lives were bereft of any colour today. He tried to take them to nearby shelter homes, but no one was ready to stop; as if they were determined to reach their home towns, come what may.

Rahul drew near the woman on whose shoulder a man was leaning and who was lagging behind the rest of the group. He asked, "Sister, why are you carrying him like this?"

"He is my husband; he has hurt his ankle and can't walk now. See how deep the wound is!"She pointed towards the injury that the man had sustained on his right foot. The man looked up at Rahul with pain in his eyes.

"But where are you going like this, especially when the condition of your husband is so bad?"

The woman sighed at this and lifted the bundle down from her head. Rahul took hold of the bundle quickly to give her some relief. The woman narrated her ordeal to Rahul. "What do I tell you! He worked as an electrician. But after the lockdown, he lost his work. I myself worked as a housemaid but they too asked me to leave. We did not have enough food at home and the landlord was also demanding rent. Food could be managed from the hunger relief centre but where could we pay the rent from? So, we had no choice but to leave for our village."

"This morning as we were walking down the road, he met with an accident and hurt his foot. Now, he is not able to walk on his own and we do not have any place to stay. So I have to carry him like this." Saying this she broke down and started crying. Her husband gave a low moan.

Overcome with grief, all he could do was to fold his hands towards Rahul. Rahul's eyes also welled up. Rahul assured them of help and said,

"We are from an NGO and are helping people who are homeless and in distress."

As the words fell on their ears, their eyes gleamed with hope. Rahul nodded at them smilingly and promised them a place in a shelter home.

"What's your name?"

"Rekha."

"Rekha... In the shelter home, you will not only get food but also medical assistance."

Rahul saw them in a fix. They looked at each other as if distressed by something. Rahul understood what it was.

"Oh, don't worry. You do not have to pay anything. The shelter is free of cost."

They agreed to the proposition. After all, how could she carry her husband like that for another 200 kms to the village while the latter was hurt and unable to walk.

By now, the driver had done the necessary repairs and the bus was ready to go. Rahul called out to Dayal Babu who was ready to board the bus and discussed Rekha's case with him. Dayal Babu called Dr Ehsan, and requested him to arrange shelter for the distressed couple. Dr Ehsan requested them to visit a shelter home set up in a nearby government school building. They took the couple along in the bus and enrolled them in the shelter home. After ensuring the safe lodging of the couple in the shelter home,

Rahul left for the hostel. On his way back, he saw countless messages from Aditi on his phone. Rahul's heart was heavy and of all times now he wanted to talk to someone. He called her up and told her about all that had happened throughout the day. Aditi also talked about the miserable conditions in the hospital. She herself was fighting a battle every day in the hospital. Rahul was fighting another battle of his own. Both were wading through tough times like warriors. They had each other's support too. They shared it all and thus made the burden that each was carrying a little lighter.

****

For Rekha and her husband, the shelter home was nothing short of a divine intervention. Now they had a roof over their heads and food in their bellies. Not only that, a doctor came and treated the injury that Rekha's husband had sustained on his ankle. They were well taken care of. A handful of teachers there helped all the inmates in ways over and above their needful duties.

This shelter home had to be set up overnight. Dr Ehsan had a tough call when the situation spiralled out of control as hundreds of people were stranded with nowhere to go. He converted a government school building into a shelter home for these people. They all were taken to the shelter home in buses during the night itself.

Sitting in his office, Dr Ehsan himself saw to it that the shelter was set up in no time. It was 10 p.m. and his phone was constantly ringing as he was planning with his team. This time, there was a call from the officers on field duty who accompanied the buses ferrying the homeless people to the shelter home. There was a law-and-order situation.

The residents of the area where the shelter home was set up were protesting and would not let the people get off the bus.

Dr Ehsan understood the gravity of the situation and was soon on his way to the shelter home. The area was throbbing with people who had gathered in front of the school gate. The sirens were blaring and police personnel were dispersing the crowd.

Dr Ehsan had to deal with the situation. He addressed the people's concerns. Where others were either sceptical or too high-handed in dealing with people, Dr Ehsan quickly understood the apprehensions in the minds of the people. He allayed the fears in people's hearts and assured them that it was not a quarantine centre but only a temporary shelter home for homeless people. The crowd dispersed and the homeless people were deboarded and rehabilitated in the school building.

Ms Sakshi, the school vice principal, was briefed about the new development. While she was anxious initially, Dr Ehsan quelled her worries and assured her of all assistance from the administration. The shelter home became a life-changing experience for the inmates, in the days to come, owing to the efforts of Ms Sakshi and her team of teachers. Such was the charisma of this young SDM that he instilled courage in the faintest of hearts. Ms Sakshi ran the shelter home so efficiently and with such a humane touch that she was titled 'Durga' by her superiors.

****

Next morning, Rahul went to check on the people in the shelter home. Rahul met Ms Sakshi who was looking after the breakfast arrangements for the inmates. Ms Sakshi told Rahul how the inmates were being provided with proper rooms with beddings, clean toilets and all the meals. She told him that among the inmates, there was a drug addict too. He was having a hard time there. But they were taking care of it all. Rahul thanked Ms Sakshi and moved ahead to check on Rekha and other inmates himself. Hardly had he walked a few steps that he saw the school head talking to a news reporter. The news reporter had turned up to cover the newly set up shelter home and the school head was going gaga over his own efforts to make this shelter home a grand success in front of the camera. Rahul was dismayed at the ways of the world. Some people like Ms Sakshi toil silently with the sole objective of serving others while many like the school head hog all the limelight without doing anything. With a knowing smile on his face Rahul hurried towards the quarters for the inmates. He saw that many homeless people stayed in the rooms of the school building. They were provided with mattresses and beddings through the district administration. Rahul went upstairs where Rekha and her husband were staying. He peeped into one of the rooms and saw Rekha sitting near the door.

As Rekha looked up, she recognised Rahul. She stood up and turned towards him with folded hands. He asked Rekha about her husband's condition.

Rekha pointed towards her husband who was lying on a mattress inside a room. His foot was bandaged. "We can't thank you enough. We are very comfortable here. A doctor also came and attended to him. It's all because of you. You are an angel sent by God," Rekha said in one breath.

Rahul felt rather embarrassed at this panegyric and made light of his own efforts.

Rekha said, "No brother, what you did for us is a great help at this time. Otherwise, who cares for others in this world."

Rahul had no words and he just stood there folding his hands in return.

Rekha further voiced her concern. "But how long can we stay like this? We have to go back to our family in the village eventually. If you could make any arrangements for us, it would be of great help."

Rahul assured her that he would soon make some arrangements to send them back to their village.

When Rahul walked back from there, he was content. It was the kind of contentment that one feels when one does something good for others without a speck of their own self-interest.

Rahul saw that the school head lodged himself back into his car and was leaving the premises. The news reporter and his entourage were nowhere to be seen too. Ms Sakshi was talking to Dr Ehsan who had just then come on his daily round to the shelter home. Rahul felt elated to see Dr Ehsan. Dr Ehsan gestured to Rahul to come over. Rahul quickly approached them.

"Rahul, have you met Ms Sakshi yet?"

"Yes sir, I had the fortune of meeting her in the morning itself."

"Oh, that's great. Look Rahul, I want you also to work in tandem with her. I see that you are quite familiar with the inmates here. Soon, we will make arrangements to send them all back to their native places. Be there and help Ms Sakshi."

"For sure, sir."

Ms Sakshi nodded her head in assent.

Rahul had gained entry into a domain where he had all the opportunity to prove useful to the society, and at the same time make a name for himself that he could never achieve had he remained confined to his mundane day-to-day life.

Rahul visited the shelter home regularly and helped in its management immensely. He worked with Ms Sakshi and her team of teachers closely. Rahul helped in raising funds for providing clothes and other essentials to the inmates. They all had become one big family by now. That was why Rahul and Ms Sakshi had tears in their eyes on the day they parted with the inmates. Buses were arranged to ferry them to their homes in different states.

Rahul sent Nathu Lal, Deviprasad, Rekha and many others like them through these buses. He had developed an association with them all. And so when the bus was about to leave, they were waving at him with eyes filled with tears. Rahul just stood there folding his hands and smiling.

Tonight, he could sleep easily. In sending Nathu Lal, Rekha and others back to their villages in this manner, he felt that a part of the lost dignity of man was thus restored; the dignity that was cruelly trampled upon when the poor and homeless were suddenly left bereft of all human rights; the dignity that was lost when many had to embark upon the journey of hundreds of kilometres on foot just because they were too poor to be cared for.

❑

7

CHAPTER

Love in the Times of Pandemic

Love is not about property, diamonds, and gifts. It is about sharing your very self with the world around you.

—Pablo Neruda

The pandemic showed no sign of abating. Since the pandemic hit, the hope of returning to normalcy was getting feebler with each passing day. People lived under constant fear. A miniscule virus had turned their lives taciturn. The period of lockdown brought many things in its wake; from social isolation and work from home to migration of labourers from cities. It was a phenomenon never seen before and one that came in many hues. In the midst of it all, there were many who were working selflessly for others. They were fighting from the front. They were the ones who were carrying the beacon of hope in these trying times. If people still had hope in humanity, it was because of those people, the frontline workers. They kept the spark of hope ignited. The hope that not all was lost; and that mankind would continue to fight this battle till the end. The frontline workers laid their own lives on the line in such a perilous situation.

Rahul had just returned from the hunger relief centre. Since Arun had an official meeting on Zoom, Manish was forbidden from turning the TV on. Rahul tiptoed into the room after taking a bath and sanitising his things. Manish was lying on the couch fiddling with a Rubik's cube. Rahul crept into the couch, gesturing Manish to make way for him. Arun had sensed Rahul's entry into the room and he signalled 'five' to him with his hand. At this, Manish put his hand over his chest and gasped indicating a sigh of relief after an unending ordeal for the last forty minutes.

As Arun's meeting was over, he turned towards Rahul and asked him about the work in the field.

"Same drill, Arun. When will this pandemic end, yaar? Everyone is jaded by now." Rahul's fingers were playing in a rapid fashion over the Rubik's cube as he spoke.

"Can't agree more. What did we know of any pandemic thing before this? I mean there had been dengue and chikungunya earlier. But who had thought that such a thing would happen as is happening now?"

"You know, Manjeet got infected with dengue when it was at its peak. But things were not so bad as they are now. Remember, Manish?" Arun continued.

"Yeah. I heard the other day that a pandemic strikes every hundred years. The last we saw was the Spanish flu in 1918. Means the next will strike around 2020," Manish spoke eruditely.

"Really? I'm sure it's yet another gem from your WhatsApp storehouse of knowledge?" Arun said in a tongue-in-cheek manner as he rose to go.

"Come on, man! It's everywhere. You can google it if you have any doubt." Manish protested.

"Here, take it." Rahul had solved the Rubik's cube by now and he threw it towards Manish who was searching for 'Spanish flu' on google.

Manish grabbed it in a flash and saw all the colours aligned in perfect symmetry.

"Wow! How did you do it, dude?" Rahul winked at him and went on with Arun.

"Rahul, I will go for the food distribution work tomorrow. You stay back and update the accounts record. Mr Balvinder was asking for it today."

"All right. If you go there, do check on Savita's family. Her husband is not well. We arranged the medicines but we need to keep a tab. Savita was overwrought."

"Oh. Don't worry, I will check on them. Hey, do you know Mr Balvinder is also running a fever? I got to know about it in the meeting today." Arun said in a concerned voice.

"What? That's alarming. I hope it's just a normal viral fever."

****

Rahul and Arun were like godsent angels to the people in the slum whom they were serving without thinking twice about their own safety. For these slum dwellers, they were the manna from heaven. All the more, as their zeal for the work came out of their own self-will. They were not coerced into this. They went about overseeing the hunger relief camp and distributing food to all the families of the slum allotted to them. Not only that, they were all ears to the problems faced by slum dwellers and always tried to resolve them.

Constantly working in this capacity, they would receive many distress calls, when until one day they got a call from unexpected quarters. This one was from their boss's wife Indu. Indu was scared beyond measure. She was so panicky that Arun could make out from her voice that something untoward had happened.

Arun asked, "What happened, ma'am? Is everything fine?"

Indu sobbed, "Balvinder ji had very high fever. He went to the washroom and slipped there. He has hurt his head badly. Please come soon. He is unconscious and I don't know what to do," she cried bitterly.

"Indu ma'am, please hold up... I'm coming."

"Oh, please come at once, Arun."

Rahul, who was sitting beside Arun, was fiddling with a ball. He gathered from Arun's conversation that something terrible had happened.

"What's the matter?" Rahul asked just when Arun hung up the phone.

"Mr Balvinder just had an accident. He has high fever too. It was his wife, Indu ji. She was crying bitterly. We need to rush."

Arun quickly swung into action. He called Ravi and told him about the accident. He asked him to make alternative arrangements at the food distribution camp where they were supposed to render their services in the morning and left for Balvinder Singh's residence. Rahul and Manjeet went there with him.

They drove and reached Balvinder Singh's residence in Kamala Nagar in 15 minutes. All three rushed to the place where Balvinder Singh lay unconscious. Balvinder Singh had high fever and he had fallen down in a delirium. His head was bleeding.

Manjeet was startled and said, "Oh, so much bleeding. We have to take him to the hospital as quickly as possible."

Indu was inconsolable. She was crying bitterly. Arun got a glass of water and solaced her. He asked Rahul to call Dr Aditi immediately.

Rahul called Aditi. "Hi, Aditi, are you at the hospital?"

Aditi replied, "Yes."

Rahul hurriedly said, "Please arrange for an emergency bed. Balvinder sir has slipped and is bleeding profusely. Moreover, he has raging fever too."

Aditi said, "Oh that's bad! Don't worry; bring him to the hospital immediately. Meanwhile, I will make arrangements here."

Rahul took the keys of the car from Indu and called out to Arun and Manjeet. They lifted the unconscious Balvinder Singh and took him to the car. As they were helping him onto the back seat, he regained consciousness and let out a feeble cry in pain.

Rahul said, "Hurry up Arun, Aditi is at the hospital only. I have asked her to help us."

Soon, the car was speeding towards City Hospital. Aditi had arranged for a stretcher at the gate. The emergency ward of the hospital bore a tumultuous look. Two ward boys rushed it to the emergency ward. Aditi helped in getting Balvinder Singh admission. The hospital was a dedicated COVID care centre and getting admission there for treatment for any non-COVID case was near impossible. But Aditi managed it all.

Balvinder Singh was bleeding profusely, and his condition was critical. Dr Aditi used her influence to make all the necessary arrangements and looked after everything personally. She also arranged for the COVID RAT test and requested Dr Nikunj, a neurosurgeon and an acquaintance of hers, for the treatment. Dr Nikunj, who was working in the trauma centre of the hospital, quickly responded to Aditi's request. Within half an hour, he was there studying the case. He instructed Aditi to run the necessary tests. The two handled it together. Dr Nikunj told Aditi that he would decide on further course of action after the test reports came in and asked her to send his report immediately. Meanwhile, the COVID RAT test of Balvinder also came positive. This was a cause of another concern. His fever was not going down.

Dr Aditi personally kept a watch on the condition of the patient while taking care of other patients too. Arun informed Balvinder Singh's wife Indu about the course of the treatment and asked her not to worry. Indu was miserable and wanted to visit the hospital. But Arun knew that Indu with her feeble nerves and gout could only make herself and others more miserable instead of providing any comfort to anyone. Moreover, it was not safe for her to visit

Balvinder who was COVID-19 positive too. He assured her that everything was being managed by them and the situation was well under control.

The other test reports came out. After analysing them, Dr Nikunj told Aditi that there was no need to operate on him but advised that the patient be kept under observation as he had a deep wound on his skull. Dr Aditi thanked Dr Nikunj for his support and he in return assured her of his support whenever required. Moreover, Aditi did not want the case to get complicated because of COVID. She deputed a ward boy to look after Balvinder Singh and share his health information timely. She asked Rahul to keep away for safety reasons.

Dr Aditi took immense pains in treating Balvinder Singh. Rahul saw exhaustion on her face as she told him and Arun about the treatment given to Balvinder Singh and asked them not to worry. She assured them that Balvinder would be fit enough to be discharged from the hospital after his full recovery.

Arun went to the reception desk to attend to paperwork leaving Rahul and Aditi together. Their eyes beheld each other. A gentleness and affection were felt by both of them. Rahul was looking at Aditi's serene face as if saying, 'I need you like a heart needs a beat'. Aditi's eyes reciprocated the feelings. 'Being with you keeps me alive and thinking about you keeps me awake'. The warmth of their fondness, the tenderness of their budding love was flaming.

What was so special about their connection? Love comes quietly without banners or flashing lights. Only those who are in love can hear the bells ringing and violins playing.

After looking into the paperwork, Arun made a call to Indu and briefed her about Balvinder's condition so that the family could be relieved from their mental anguish. The boys were also relaxed. Rahul had decided to stay back at the hospital at night. Arun and Manjeet left for Goyal House. Meanwhile, Aditi arranged for his stay at the hospital. She came to visit the emergency ward. Rahul was sitting outside and she called him.

"Rahul, will you have a cup of coffee?"

Rahul said, "Oh yes, I'll have. I am very tired. Adu, how do you manage everything so well?"

Aditi was jubilant hearing herself addressed as Adu. "Hey, you just called me Adu. Oh, that sounded so much better. And Rahul, I manage things the same way as you do."

A smile played across Rahul's face. Aditi's cheeks had turned crimson. There was a kind of strong magnetic pull that attracted them towards each other irrespective of themselves. They both smiled with a twinkle in their eyes. The true meaning of love is not understood until it's found. True love isn't the fairytale which all are led to believe as kids, but the unbelievably strong bond that forms as one travels through life with someone and faces great joys and deep sorrows. True love is not meant to be perfect; it's complicated and enduring. And it comes when it is least expected.

Rahul took Aditi's hand and held it between his own hands. Aditi looked up into his deep and thoughtful eyes gazing intently at her. He was rubbing her dainty hands and his gaze, set upon her face, conveyed his solicitude towards her. Aditi did not need any words from Rahul to understand how concerned he was for her and how much he wanted her to get away from that mad rush of the hospital in which she was caught up day and night. Rahul had very intent eyes and the way they looked sharply at something made him look so irresistibly strong in character that Aditi was smitten by them.

Rahul said, "If you weren't there..." But even before he could finish his sentence, he was cut short by Aditi. "And why would that be so? Let us go and have some coffee. It's been long since we had a chance to sit together."

Aditi took Rahul by hand to the duty room. Rahul sat down on the sofa lying in a corner. Aditi made a call and ordered two coffees. She put the phone receiver back and removed her coat. Throwing her coat on the back of the chair, she jumped onto the sofa beside Rahul. She leaned back out of the utter exhaustion of unending duty hours. Rahul rubbed her shoulder as Aditi went on talking about the ordeal she faced the whole day, owing to the breakdown of healthcare facilities in the face of the onslaught of the pandemic. Rahul kept comforting her with his loving care and patient hearing. He told her about the work he was doing through the NGO.

The coffee arrived and Rahul took the tray. Aditi was quite hungry by now. She stopped the ward boy who had turned back to leave.

"Wait... wait, just wait... Hey Rahul I'm so hungry, would you like to have some snacks also?"

"Yeah, let's get something."

"Alright, bring whatever snacks are available. Should be good." Aditi's words were directed at the ward boy.

"Yes ma'am," saying these words, he opened the door and left. Soon he was back with burgers and rolls. Rahul and Aditi chatted over the cups of coffee and ate to their heart's content. Rahul always thought of Aditi to be of a more serious disposition, but tonight he saw her bubbly and childlike self. He sat there and listened to her. He laughed at every funny thing she said and listened gravely to every serious word of hers.

Aditi was tired and she put her head over Rahul's shoulder. Soon, she dozed off. Rahul did not budge lest he wake her up. He supported her with his arm and gently leaned back on the sofa. There could not be anything more beautiful than this for Rahul. There could not be anything more relaxing either. How much he wished that night to last forever. Rahul too closed his eyes. All the consciousness that he had in his being was just there at the spot of his shoulder and neck where he could feel Aditi on his body. His whole being and existence revelled in that sensation. The warmth of her body was melting his being. The scent of her dense and dark mane had sent his heart racing. Never had he felt any woman this close. He saw her glowing face looking all the more attractive as it laid there on his shoulder. It was hard to sit motionless while an intense desire to hold and hug her was raging within him. The sleeping beauty slumbered on his shoulders. Rahul dozed off.

It was 5 a.m. when Dr Nikunj entered the room. As he looked towards the sofa, Rahul straightened himself and looked back at him. This sudden movement woke up Aditi who had drowsed on Rahul's shoulder all through the night.

"Aditi, can we talk for two minutes?" Dr Nikunj went outside, leaving the door swinging behind him. Aditi stretched herself and looked at Rahul smilingly. "Wait here," she whispered and swiftly went out.

Nikunj first discussed the case of Balvinder with Aditi in a matter-of-fact way. But when he could no longer hold it back, he asked her straight away,

"What was that, Aditi? Who is he? Since when is this going on?"

"What's going on? Nothing. He is just a friend of mine." Aditi did not want to reveal her feelings to anyone before she could herself comprehend them completely. Nikunj's father was a family friend. She did not want anyone to know about this beautiful phase that she was going through. It was a secret that she was hiding dearly in her heart like a well-kept treasure. She did not want a row in her family over this issue. Aditi came from a respectable family with high standards of conduct and aspirations to match.

Her father had established a name for himself in the city. Mr Rajender was a self-made businessman and encouraged his children to work hard. He believed in action rather than fate. He usually said, "You can win the world through hard work." At the age of twenty-four, he married Asha who hailed from a traditional family. She was a religious woman with decent education. This marriage bore them three children. Aditi was the second of the three. Her elder sister Kaveri was also beautiful like her. She was a professor of Economics at Delhi University. Her inclination towards social causes like eradication of poverty and unemployment made her associate herself with some NGOs too. Her younger brother Nishant was still in school. He was in class 12. Aditi had always been a bright student. She fulfilled the expectations of her family by securing admission in a reputed medical college.

Nikunj looked at her in disbelief. He could tell that Aditi was in love after all. But he had no time to spare in questioning her further. He grew impatient. So, he just briefed her about the next course of treatment and tests to be done and left. Aditi went back in the room and found Rahul reading *The Fault in our Stars*.

"Hey, that seems pretty interesting! You like that?" Aditi excitedly came closer and peeped over

Rahul's shoulder. "It's good, yes. But I have not finished it yet."

"Lend this one to me when you're finished."

"No. I have a different one for you." Rahul rummaged through his bag and brought out a copy of *The Citadel* by A J Cronin.

"Hmm. Never heard of it. But I will surely read it. Thank you!"

Aditi quickly put her coat on, tied her hair in a bun, took the stethoscope from the table and left the room in a hurry.

It took Balvinder Singh three full weeks to recover completely. The wound on his head had healed and he had recovered from COVID as well. These three weeks were one of the most memorable ones for Rahul. His love with Aditi blossomed in the unlikeliest of places. In that grim hospital building, Rahul and Aditi grew closer to each other; sometimes in the duty room and sometimes in the empty corridors of the building. They were in an impassioned and secretive love. They could not get enough of each other. Rahul made it a point that he was the one to stay behind in the hospital at night. Arun and Manjeet would visit during the day. They knew the reason for Rahul's nightly stays at hospital.

A week before Balvinder was discharged from the hospital, Rahul went to his room and checked up on him. He was sleeping under the influence of the drugs pumped into his veins. He was cured of the disease, but the wound needed a few more days to heal. As the nurse came for the routine check-up, Balvinder rose from his slumber. He saw Rahul standing by his side. As he tried to raise himself up, he whimpered in pain. Rahul quickly supported him in his strong arms and helped in sitting up.

"You were here during the night?" asked Balvinder.

"Don't worry. The doctor has said you're fine and you are going home soon." Rahul assured him.

"Get some rest, son. You're doing so much for me." Balvinder was overwhelmed with Rahul's devotion.

Just then, Dr Aditi entered and said, "Correct Balvinder ji, he was up the whole night. You are lucky to have him by your side." Balvinder's eyes welled up at this. Aditi checked his parameters and gave some instructions to the nurse on duty. Manjeet and Arun also entered the room at this moment. Arun asked Rahul to leave and get some rest back home, but Rahul was insistent on staying back. Rahul gave way only when Balvinder himself ordered him to go home sternly.

As Rahul was leaving the hospital, he heard Aditi's voice calling him from behind. Rahul looked back and saw

Aditi running towards him. She had changed into a pair of jeans and a T-shirt. Her svelte figure was all too visible. Rahul could not help but look at her.

"Can you drop me home?" Aditi asked smilingly.

"Of course. The pleasure is all mine, madam." Rahul said with a wink.

Rahul kick-started the bike and Aditi sat behind him. Soon, both were speeding through the roads of Delhi. Aditi's hands slid from Rahul's shoulders to his waist. She could feel his tall and strong frame in her hands. She felt that with this tall man of hers, she could ride through all the ups and downs of life easily. Rahul felt a strange sensation running through his body at the touch of her hands on his back. He was in love with this woman sitting behind him. The surge of emotions broke out in the form of words.

"Adu, you know. I got so worried when Balvinder ji was down with the fever. He is such a nice person. I always see my Baba's image in him. He trusts Arun and me for every job. You see, there are very few people in this world who invest their faith in novices like us," Rahul said.

"Yes Rahul, I wonder people like him exist in this world even today. But don't worry, he will get well soon. He is a strong man with a golden heart," exclaimed Aditi.

"Aditi, I have something to say. I don't know how you will feel about me after this. But I can't hold it back anymore."

"Hmmmm." Aditi came closer and put her chin over his shoulder.

"Aditi, I like you a lot! I mean I like you as a person... the way you are you know! Yeah! I mean I really admire you..." Rahul could not really bring himself to utter those magical words after all. His heart was racing.

"Oh! Thanks! I also admire you a lot, Rahul." Aditi knew what Rahul wanted to say and she was smiling too. Not so much because of the way Rahul was ruffled but more because he had those feelings for her which he could not dress up in words so well. Those same feelings that Aditi too could feel blossoming within her for him. She savoured this moment, smiling to herself with her cheek laid gently against his back.

Rahul was on the top of the world. There was nothing more he could ask for from life. His happiness knew no bounds. He wanted to carry Aditi far away where they could be together without a care in the world.

They were breezing through the road when Rahul's attention was caught by a camp pitched in the Faculty of Arts grounds.

"What's going on over there?" Rahul alluded to the roadside camp.

"That's a blood donation camp," Aditi told him.

"A blood donation camp in this scenario?" Rahul asked apprehensively.

"In fact, in the present scenario, it's all the more needed, Rahul." Aditi went on talking about its merit. Rahul always loved listening to Aditi even though at times he would lose the thread of the conversation. Rahul brought the bike to a halt on the roadside and looked back at Aditi over his shoulder. Aditi got down and looked at Rahul questioningly.

"Aditi, what if we also set up a blood donation camp?" Rahul's eyes were brimming with excitement.

"Yes, but who will arrange..." Aditi was still unable to comprehend what had suddenly come over Rahul.

"Don't worry about that! I know someone who can help us with this." Rahul said confidently. He took out his phone and dialled Dr Ehsan's number.

Dr Ehsan quickly assented to Rahul's suggestion of organising a blood donation camp and promised administerial support in this. He suggested that it could be arranged at the SDM office itself. The following days were marked with a flurry of activities. The hostel was abuzz with the preparations for the camp. Calls were made to people and coordination was done with Dr Ehsan's team. SDM office called the hospital authorities to depute doctors and other medical staff for the camp. Anjali and Arun convinced their office staff to join in the noble cause. Rahul and Dr Aditi were busy arranging the medical team and other logistic support.

On D-day, the blood donation camp was inaugurated by Dr Ehsan, SDM at his office premises. Rahul was constantly by his side looking into every little detail. Aditi was supervising everything. The Goyal House boys and the office staff ardently joined the camp to donate blood.

Dr Ehsan was happy with the work done by Rahul and appreciated his team. Rahul was filled with gratitude.

Arun was glad that after all, Rahul was winning admiration. Aditi's heart was full of pride, love and admiration for her lover.

❑

8

CHAPTER

New Beginnings

It's not about ideas. It's about making ideas happen.
—Scott Belsky

Balvinder Singh knew very well what it meant to build everything from scratch. When lockdown perpetrated conditions, where lay-offs and shut downs became the order of the day, he adopted a rather sympathetic approach towards his employees in the beginning. He paid them in full for as long as he could. But this did not go on for too long and as his firm went into losses due to the lockdown, the workers began facing cuts in their salaries. Rahul faced this too. The uncertainties of the time and dwindling earnings were taking a toll on his morale. Especially so, after he and Aditi were together and looking at a new phase of their lives. Rahul knew that in order to deserve Aditi, he had to prove himself worthy of her. To make a place for himself, especially at times like these, was a tall order. Rahul was beset with self-doubt. After seeing Dr Nikunj in the hospital and his closeness with Aditi, Rahul had become restless. He wanted to carve a niche for himself and prove himself suitable for Aditi more than ever. He could not think of losing her to anyone.

Rahul was lost in these thoughts when Arun, who was sitting beside him on the sofa, nudged him.

"Where are you lost, man? Your phone has been ringing."

"Oh! It's nothing."

Rahul saw Dr Ehsan's name flashing on the screen. He sprang up and quickly took the call.

"Hello, Rahul. Hope I am not disturbing you at this time..."

"Not at all, sir. Please tell me what I can do."

"Rahul, if possible, try to arrange a bus to transport five girls who live in a paying guest accommodation in your area to their homes."

"Sure, sir. I will make the necessary arrangements straight away."

"Good. I am messaging you all the details. And you'll go a long way, boy."

With these words, Dr Ehsan bolstered the spirits of a dejected Rahul. His self-confidence got the much-needed boost.

The lockdown might have come as a solace for the individuals having a fast paced life in Delhi, but for the economy it was backbreaking. Many people suffered the setbacks of the economic slowdown. Rahul was a witness to it all. He saw the exodus of a large floating population of migrants on foot. Working concertedly with the NGO and Dr Ehsan's team, he was helping people in distress too. At the time when the world had turned bleak for the destitute, Rahul and Arun were the good Samaritans who worked selflessly to help others. In this manner, they were laboriously working at various fronts. Shuttling between shelter homes and NGOs, they were up and running at providing food, masks and sanitisers to the indigent.

Their work at the forefront had garnered them notability of sorts too. The blood donation camp organised by them in concert with the Sub-Divisional Magistrate, Dr Ehsan was another feather in their cap. It was the talk of the town and covered locally in the newspapers too. Rahul's self- doubt was completely unjustified. But the times were beset with so much uncertainty that sometimes even the ever-poised Rahul became too critical of himself and succumbed to self- doubt. But he recovered and became stronger in his resolve to prove himself.

Just as Rahul and Arun were persistently involved in their altruistic acts, Aditi too was assiduously working and had to spend long hours, unflaggingly at the hospital. Aditi was completely unaware of Rahul's insecurities in respect to Dr Nikunj. Aditi had never entertained Nikunj as anything more than an acquaintance. Rahul and Aditi could not find much time to spend with each other. Throughout the lockdown, their relationship saw spells of affection and indifference.

Whereas business activities had suffered badly and all the big and small business enterprises were knocked down, Balvinder Singh's import-export business had also come to a standstill. His publishing house work was closed too. Many employees quit their jobs and went to their native places. Meanwhile, the pandemic showed no sign of abating.

Nothing good had happened to Balvinder Singh since the lockdown. As if all this was not enough, now the medical bills had broken his back after his illness. Although he had recovered and was back home, and Indu was thankful to God for saving her husband's life, Balvinder had other worries. He was facing a dire situation. On the one hand his health was failing ever since he had a brush with COVID, and on the other hand his finances were dwindling. He experienced fatigue and muscular pain very often. He had lost his strength not just physically, but mentally too.

One day, a disconsolate Balvinder was sitting at the breakfast table brooding over his depreciating financial condition. It was then that one of his close friends and business aides Roshan Singh called up. He had perceived the market demand and, in response, had started a wholesale business of masks, sanitisers and thermal scanners. The two discussed the business and Balvinder realised how profitable the venture had proved for Roshan Singh. Roshan Singh suggested Balvinder try his hands at something like that. The discussion with Roshan Singh proved serendipitous to Balvinder. He had a great business idea that he knew he could easily pull off. Balvinder deliberated over it for long and when he discussed it with his wife Indu, she too found the business proposition quite promising.

When Balvinder called Arun, he had his plans. Arun picked up the phone and surprisingly found Balvinder, his old cheerful self again. Balvinder sounded quite elated.

"Hey! Arun, where is Rahul? Call him and put the phone on speaker."

Arun called Rahul, who was on the balcony sipping on his cup of coffee.

Balvinder Singh discussed the new business idea with Arun and Rahul. It was a business venture involving supply of essentials such as sanitisers, masks, PPE kits, oximeters and thermal scanners.

Rahul and Arun were happy that Balvinder sounded cheerful long after his corona stint. They both exclaimed, “That’s a great idea and the need of the hour, sir. What do you want from us?”

Balvinder continued, “I want you both to join me. See, I can’t carry on anymore with all this work pressure. But a constant source of income must be there. I am too frail now and who would look after this business empire that I have erected after me? You two are like sons to me. So what I have in mind is that you look after this firm and run it. You will have a 50 percent partnership in this enterprise.” I will make the initial investment too.

Rahul and Arun couldn’t believe their ears. They were being offered a 50 percent partnership. They were too startled to say anything. Each thought that Mr Balvinder was being delusional post his illness. They looked at each other in surprise.

“Arun? Are you listening?” Balvinder inquired.

“Umm... yes, I’m listening.” Arun could barely bring himself to utter these words.

Rahul probed Balvinder on this. “Sir, are you talking about partnership? If we heard it right.”

"Yes, yes my son!" Balvinder guffawed. "The basement of our office is quite spacious and vacant too. You can use it to set up everything required. And yes, you heard it right; you'll have a 50 percent partnership. Give me my 50 percent but mind you, I am not going to do anything. I'm an old and weak man now. You will have my basement. That's all. It will be a profitable start-up for you if you manage to make it work. Go ahead, my boys! Make money out of it. Good luck!"

After the call, Arun and Rahul gave each other a big high five. The world was for theirs to take. They could never have imagined getting an opportunity like that. None could, in fact! But good fortune doesn't shy away for long from those who work hard in a systematic and planned way.

Out of all his employees, Balvinder wanted to rope in Arun and Rahul for this new venture. The two had completely won his trust. Balvinder was well aware of their loyalty and dedication. They too were excited at this offer. With the business being shut down, their income was cut by half. They knew very well that to be able to stay afloat in a metropolitan city like Delhi the income must consistently flow in, otherwise the day would not be far when they too would have to pack their bags and leave. Delhi is a harbour for people coming in from all walks of life and all corners of the country. But the same city can prove to be quite harsh when things go wrong as was the case with migrant labourers.

Rahul was on cloud nine. The disturbing thoughts of the past days of being unworthy of Aditi and being lesser than Nikunj gave way to the hope of a brighter future. With this new-found confidence, he called Aditi to break the news to her. Arun too called Anjali to share this. After all, the butterflies were going to emerge from their chrysalises to spread their wings and fill their world with colours.

Over the next two weeks, Rahul and Arun were running from pillar to post, setting up the new firm. They completed all the necessary documentation and registration work. The firm had to supply essential items to government offices, pharmacy shops, hospitals and the NGOs working in its jurisdiction. Rahul and Arun contacted the officials and convinced them about the quality and timely supply of the items. Finally, they had found the foundation stone for a firm footing on the business scene of Delhi. They became the new emerging entrepreneurs.

In the course of a month, the manufacturing and distribution firm of essentials took off at full throttle. They roped in more people in this venture, which was not too hard, as due to the sudden lockdown many had lost their work. Arun even called a few of his friends to join the firm.

Rahul had by now established himself well in Delhi. The new business grew like wildfire. The conditions were suitable and demand was very high. Therefore, the stocks kept disappearing from the shelves fast. It was just the right thing. Rahul managed everything well. He made the most of his technical knowledge in execution of this new work that he was entrusted to. A WhatsApp group was created where people could place online orders too.

Balvinder Singh invested an initial sum of twenty lakh rupees in this venture. He gave Rahul and Arun the space for running the firm. The rest was managed completely by

Rahul and Arun. Arun was handling the manpower and demand-supply chain management part of the new business while Rahul was entrusted with marketing, accounts and finances. It was ushering in a new beginning for them.

Even at a very nascent stage, they received an order worth seven lakh rupees. They managed to deliver it too, though it required an immense amount of effort to procure the material and deliver it in a timely manner. But all this effort was put in by Arun and Rahul who left no stone unturned. The business flourished and so did their dreams.

Time flew; life began to return to normalcy. The government had lifted restrictions as the number of active cases reduced. People started flocking back on deserted roads again. They were slowly returning to their work. But the struggle to save life was still on. Corona cases were ebbing day by day in Delhi. From the relief camps to the shelter homes, the crowds gradually started dispersing. But people could still be seen queuing up at the ration shops. The impact of the pandemic was not restricted to the cities. The pandemic was slowly percolating down to every nook and corner of the country. The shop where Rahul's father used to work had been closed since the lockdown. The owner of the shop paid his father one month's salary in lockdown. But after one month, he was unable to pay full salary. So, from the second month onwards he reduced the salary to half. The ₹ 2,000-instalment given under the Kisan Samman Nidhi to the farmers by the government of India somehow helped his father to manage the household expenses.

Rahul found out about the hardships of his family when he made a call home. Though Amma and Baba did not talk so openly about their problems, it was not difficult for Rahul to figure it all out. Amma was worried about the well-being of her son who was miles away from home, living in a new city which was engulfing people in its death jaws. They knew that big cities like Delhi were hotspots of death and people were facing all kinds of troubles since the lockdown. They implored him to come back. But Rahul had other plans. Rahul knew how to make the most out of any situation. He had come to Delhi to carve a niche for himself. The current situation did not deter his ambitions at all. Rather, he was bolder in his intent than ever. He had never been the one to run away from any situation. How could he do so now when at last, he began to feel he was getting a firm hold in the city! The time was ripe to establish himself in the business. Rahul, the elder one, bearing all the responsibilities since childhood, was always like this. Everyone trusted him, from parents to teachers; and now this city, and the people therein.

During the time of the pandemic, when no one was there with Balvinder Singh, both Rahul and Arun stayed with him day and night. They were there with him through thick and thin. They were looking after the new business and worked like horses. Rahul's world had suddenly spun into one that he could never have imagined in the wildest of his dreams. It was only yesterday that he moved to the city and adapted himself to it. He toiled in the office and established himself in the new workplace. By the time Rahul found his feet in the city, everything came to a halt. Business was bad, shutters were down, and people were losing their jobs.

But he was not one to bow down to anything. He emerged stronger than ever. If sacrifices had to be made for it, so be it. Rahul was ready.

****

After the lockdown struck, most of the boys in the hostel had left for their hometowns. Now only six out of the twenty-five boys remained. The cook too had left. But food was not an issue for them anymore. One day, while they were busy in the preparations of their dinner, they received a distress call. Arun picked up and heard the anxious voice of a girl.

"Hello! Hello, sir. Are you... Mr Arun?"

"Yes, I am. Who are you?" Arun asked.

The girl had got Arun's number through someone who had worked in a hunger relief centre. Her father, who used to do odd jobs, was the sole breadwinner in the family. Now that he had lost his job, the family's condition had deteriorated so much that they were on the brink of starvation. The girl narrated her ordeal to Arun in one breath. Since they had migrated to Delhi from another state, they didn't have any ration card. Without a ration card, they could not get any share of dry ration. The meagre amount of food provided at the hunger relief centre was not enough to feed a family of thirteen members. Arun assured her of help. "Sir, if there is any work for me, I will do it. It hurts me a lot when I beg for help. We are poor but not beggars. I can work to feed my family. Sir, my mother and I can work as house help too," pleaded the girl.

Hunger and dignity cannot go hand in hand. The lack of work and loss of jobs had not hit people in one way. It had laid the frailty of human existence exposed. People were helpless and the dignity of life was threatened.

Arun was in a fix as to how to help the family. There were no jobs. The family lived in another part of Delhi. It was not feasible for them to provide rations to this family. Arun discussed it with Rahul and Manish. Together they came upon an idea. They asked the girl to purchase the household supplies from her local store and Arun made the payment through Paytm. Technology reaches everywhere and opens vistas that are not possible in other conventional ways. If there is any significant revolution in the world since the industrial revolution, it is the technological revolution. In such myriad ways, Rahul and Arun were helping people living in distress.

****

A cloud of dust rose in the old building compound of the SDM office when a white Innova with a beacon screeched to a halt. Dr Ehsan alighted. There was a hint of fatigue in his countenance. Since morning, he had attended three consecutive meetings. His phone was ringing ceaselessly. He dashed to his room while blurting instructions to his subordinates. The workload had increased exponentially and he had to work round the clock. Dr Ehsan was a doctor by education, but the charm of serving people had brought him into administrative services. No one could understand the gravity of the pandemic situation better than him. He was a young and enthusiastic officer ready to scale heights and face challenges. A one-man army, Dr. Ehsan believed in team work and motivated his workforce by way of example. His ardour for his work was evident in his bearing. The dullness that the civil servants often fall prey to, with advancing years in service, has not had any impact on him yet. The sharpness of intellect and humility in conduct had made him a favourite with people. He didn't carry the impregnable aura around him that other officers often would. People would approach him directly when they were in distress. This agreeableness in his own character sometimes vexed him. He felt that this had left him with no private space of his own; where he could be himself and play with his one-year-old son, without a care in the world. Sometimes he yearned for a laidback life with his family. Since the pandemic struck, he was working round the clock.

Before the fatigue turned into exasperation, he recollected himself and started working on the new night shelter that was set up instantaneously in his jurisdiction. The night shelter was home to more than a hundred vagabonds and pavement dwellers who had no work and no place to turn to. Dr Ehsan was engrossed in his work when the phone rang. There were many calls from this number this morning.

Dr Ehsan had just settled in his seat after the meeting when the phone rang again. The call was from the same number.

"Sorry to disturb you, sir. But we are really thankful for the way you helped us out of the situation we were in." It was a girl's voice.

Dr Ehsan could not exactly recollect who this obliged person was now. After the countless incidents of assistance to people, it was not easy to recollect them all. "Oh sir, I guess you don't remember me. Just a few days ago, I had reached out to you for help as the landlord was hounding us for payment of rent. You set things right and sent Rahul to arrange a bus for us on our way back home."

"Oh yes. Now I do recollect. I hope everything is resolved by now."

"Perfectly, sir! That's why I called to thank you."

Dr Ehsan had helped this group of five girls who lived in a paying guest accommodation in Shalimar Bagh, Delhi. Three other girls who were staying there left the place when the lockdown hit. Later, they refused to pay the rent owed by them. The landlord was forcing the remaining five girls to cover the other three's rent too. The girls could only pay what was owed by them. Thereafter, they did not even have the money to return home.

Many such problems arose in the atypical circumstances that the pandemic brought with itself. For him, all of this had become the order of day by now. Dr Ehsan was happy with the way Rahul was proving useful, every time he was needed.

After this call, he leaned back in his chair and closed his eyes. Rahul's face was floating before his eyes. His ambitiousness and zestfulness in particular, charmed him every time he met him. But what fascinated him the most was that somehow he saw a semblance of himself in Rahul. He remembered those last days in college when everyone else was exhilarated at the prospect of becoming doctors. But he himself was not content with just that. His ambitiousness and the will to serve as an IAS officer was driving him to a new uncharted path. Just like Rahul, his own ambition and verve were uncontainable. The way Rahul was working hard to make a place for himself in a distant land, Dr Ehsan had done so a decade ago. He could clearly remember that first day in office which marked a new beginning of his career as a civil servant.

❑

9

CHAPTER

Various Shades of Love

In vain have I struggled. It will not do.
My feelings will not be repressed.
You must allow me to tell you how ardently
I admire and love you.

—Jane Austen

It was the month of August. The protracted lockdown had a healing touch on Mother Nature. Within a few months of lockdown, there were tangible changes in the environment. One such morning, Aditi woke up to a beautiful sight. A couple of sparrows were chirping on her window sill. Their wings were glistening in the golden sunlight. Only a couple of decades ago or so, sparrows used to be in abundance in Delhi. But with rising pollution levels and high degree of urbanisation, sparrows gradually disappeared from the scene of Delhi. This unusual sighting of sparrows delighted Aditi. She felt as if this was an indication of something good that was about to happen. Rahul's face was hovering before her. Somehow, the radiant morning rays, the chirping of sparrows, and the cool breeze gently touching her cheeks, were all making her think about Rahul. It was as if all her thoughts revolved around him only. Never had she felt herself so irresistibly drawn towards someone. She called him up.

It was 6 in the morning. After a few rings Rahul picked up the call, half asleep. He didn't notice whose call it was.

"Hello? Who is this?" Rahul mumbled. His voice sent a thrill in her body.

"Oh. So now you don't even recognise me," she taunted him playfully.

"Aditi, it's you! I was just sleeping. Who else can have such a mellifluous voice? It's a pleasure to wake up to your voice. And, to what do I owe the pleasure of your call?" Rahul asked, making up for the initial mess.

Hearing that compliment from him, her smile broadened. Of course, she wanted to tell him that the pleasure was all hers. But her spirited self did not let her do that. She continued with her friendly banter and told him that he didn't need to cover up.

It was too early in the morning for a rendezvous but Aditi couldn't wait. She told him that she had just returned from her night shift and was in no mood to sleep. Rahul was also burning with passion. He seized the opportunity and asked her if she would like to go for a walk in the Ridge area. He had never asked a girl out and he didn't know how Aditi would react. His question had been impromptu. Aditi loved listening to his deep husky voice. She was overjoyed at Rahul's move. In her ecstasy, the thoughts of what to wear started running in her mind. Nowadays, she wanted to look her best in front of Rahul as if it ever mattered to him. What attracted him the most was her simplicity and innocence, her beautiful eyes which did a lot of talking even when she wasn't saying a word. She forgot that she had to respond. Rahul was thinking of apologising to Aditi when she suddenly replied in the affirmative.

Rahul jumped off his bed. "Where shall I pick you up?" he asked and then controlled his excitement lest it play spoilsport.

"Just outside my hostel," Aditi said, hiding her excitement.

"I'll be there in no time." He disconnected the phone in a hurry because he too wanted to look his best. Though she was attracted to his looks as well, yet it was his humility and intelligence that made her fall head over heels in love with him. Rahul reached outside her hostel and sent her a message that he was waiting outside. She looked out of the window and there he was; his eyes never leaving hers. His eyes were mesmerising and provocative at the same time. They were black with a hint of gold and coincidentally, matched his hair. She knew she was staring but he was staring back. Feeling awkward but a little flattered, she politely looked away and ran downstairs.

As Rahul saw her, he was awestruck. She had the perfect features, with her enchanting eyes, nose, and ears, well proportioned and set perfectly on her face. Her tiny bindi matched her pale yellow and white salwar kameez. She looked like Alia Bhatt's smarter cousin if there was such a possibility.

"Hi." Rahul initiated a conversation without breaking his gaze. His eyes were still drinking the nectar of her beauty and simplicity. He kept on looking at the divinely beautiful girl and could still not believe that he was the lucky one. He pinched himself and stole a glance at her again before asking her to sit behind him on his bike.

"Hey," Aditi replied with a smile on her face and happiness in her eyes.

As they reached the Ridge area, Rahul parked his bike on the side of the road and while walking, the melodious chirping of birds was like a piece of background music for them. The one good thing that came out of lockdown was that Mother Earth had started healing herself. The sky was clearer, the air was better; it seemed like everything had been washed anew.

Aditi watched the captivating clouds slide over the bright blue sky, while Rahul was looking at her face. To him, she was nothing less than a perfectly sculpted piece of art. As they walked silently appreciating nature's beauty, Rahul said, "Look how everything has changed, I have never seen the Delhi sky so clear and bright."

Aditi replied, "Cannot agree more. It seems Earth is healing itself. Pollution levels have never been so low. Air quality couldn't have been better."

The beauty of that August day was almost staggering. With the monsoon splattering its water droplets, everything that could turn green had outdone itself in greenness and everything that could even dream of blooming or blossoming was in bloom and blossom. The sunlight was a benediction. The breeze was so caressingly soft and intimate on the skin as to be embarrassing.

They took off down a path covered softly with moss and tiny pink flowers. Off to the side of the path were endless green trees and plants all nestled together to make one beautiful piece of art. After a while, they reached a garden with a sparkling, clear lake. The path wound right alongside the water. Walking along the lake, they noticed the wind was beginning to blow a little faster now, and they could hear the steady, rushing noise of the water.

Rahul didn't know what came over him, whether it was the weather, the breeze, the sound of water or the feelings he had for Aditi. He slightly moved his hand to hold Aditi. The sudden touch made her crimson and she reciprocated by holding his hand back. They silently held each other's hands and continued walking. Those few moments without uttering a word conveyed their feelings for each other. Aditi slightly bent and put her head on his shoulders. His heart was full of desire to hug her tight, right then and there.

They walked in silence cherishing this lovely moment which had come after a long time. Rahul kissed her fingers. She snuggled into him.

****

Freedom entails responsibility. An unconditional freedom often culminates in anarchy. When India finally decided to lift the lockdown in a staggered manner, the freedom that it was going to allow its people was full of apprehensions and fears. What if the people used this freedom to move around, in an irresponsible way?

The administration was staring at such possibilities. The government lifted some of the restrictions while at the same time geared up the administration for the challenges ahead. For people, it came as a sigh of relief, an experience of liberation, from a long interval of captivity.

The earth healed, nature blossomed and love bloomed during the lockdown. This was not going to last forever. The lifting of restrictions made people irresponsible too. Respite proved short-lived as the situation gradually deteriorated and Delhi witnessed another surge in COVID cases around September. The whole situation was vexing. But to Rahul and Arun's business, it provided further impetus as demand for masks, sanitisers and disinfectants increased further. While the corona was raging, their business was flourishing.

Dr Aditi also got busy as the hospitals again began to witness increasing emergencies. Her duty hours increased again. This was a setback for her. She was preparing for her NEET PG exam scheduled early next year. But as the situation got worse, she was not left with enough time to study for it. At times, she would become frustrated. But Rahul was always there for her and would keep lifting her spirits.

On an October afternoon, Aditi was quite frustrated after her long duty hours. As she came back from the hospital, she received a video call from Rahul.

"Hey... how are you?" Rahul looked cheerful as he always did whenever he saw Aditi's face.

"Not good, of course." Aditi lamented. She looked exhausted.

"Oh... what happened? Are you okay?" Rahul looked worried.

"How can one be okay when one has to work the whole day? How is it even possible for me to study for my exam in this condition?" Aditi was frustrated.

Rahul tried to cheer her up. He asked her out for coffee. Aditi expressed her inability due to workload. But Rahul, the charmer, would always have a trick or two up his sleeves. They decided to have coffee at Hogwarts, their favourite rendezvous point.

Aditi looked radiant in her yellow sweatshirt and a straight skirt. She was looking taller than usual in her heeled ankle boots. Rahul couldn't take his eyes off her as she entered the cafe. She sat across from him smiling back at him. Her side-swept hair cascaded down her right shoulder. Rahul held her hand lovingly and asked her what she would like to have. Smallest gestures like a latte heart design in the coffee mug that Rahul would secretly make the cafe attendant serve to Aditi, would melt her heart and bring a smile on her face. After coffee, Rahul would drop Aditi back to the hospital on his bike. It became like a daily ritual for them. Their romantic trysts at the cafe were going unhindered like this. Until the day they were spotted by the one who coveted Aditi secretly.

Dr Nikunj was getting into his car in the hospital parking lot, when he saw Aditi alighting from Rahul's bike. While he was already seething on spotting them together yet again, it exasperated him when Aditi gave Rahul a hug. His anger knew no bounds and he felt betrayed even though he had never confessed his feelings to Aditi, and Aditi never professed any love for him either.

Nikunj was apprehensive about this little affair between Aditi and Rahul right from the beginning. He felt angry with Aditi and wanted to confront her on this.

Dr Nikunj turned back and slammed the car door. He moved towards Aditi, who was walking towards the hospital entrance with a spring in her step and a smile on her face. She saw Dr Nikunj walk towards her. She was alarmed by the expression on his face.

"Aditi, you can't fool the world, you know." His expressions were stiff in a bid to hide all his emotions except those of anger.

"What? I don't understand you. Who am I fooling?" Aditi could not understand what he was saying and was taken aback at the suddenness with which she was confronted.

"I just saw that boy you are going around with. Would you still say there is nothing going between you two? What does it all mean? How can you behave like that? Who is he?" Dr Nikunj blurted everything out in a contemptuous tone as he couldn't restrain himself any longer.

Aditi was hurt and angry at this sudden bombardment of questions on her by the very supercilious Nikunj. "What right do you have to question me like this? It's my life and I will do as I like."

It was a blow to Dr Nikunj's sense of pride. He haughtily apologised and said that he wouldn't bother her ever. It was a mistake that he had made. Dr Nikunj walked away. Aditi was agitated at this inconvenient and embarrassing encounter. That day she felt that Nikunj's overtures all these years were more than simple acts of friendliness.

Aditi was disturbed the whole day. She didn't say anything to Rahul, thinking it was a one-off incident that had passed. But it was far from being over. Dr Nikunj disclosed Rahul and Aditi's affair to her father.

That day Aditi was summoned home by her father. After finishing her work at the hospital she reached home. Aditi had a long conversation with her father after dinner. He was disturbed on hearing about his daughter's relationship with a boy who had no standing in life. He looked at her angrily and asked her about the boy she was meeting regularly. The disappointment was evident on his face. Aditi, who was looking down all this while as her father said those bitter words to her, finally looked up.

She looked imploringly at him and began,

"Papa, I have done nothing wrong. The boy, Nikunj has told you about, is Rahul. He is a very decent boy. Trust me, you'll really like him when you meet him. You know very well that I will never do anything that will jeopardise your standing in society. I'll never let you down, Papa."

"Aditi, I know you. But at your age, people do make mistakes. Don't become blinded by some passing fancy and let your life go to waste. Decency is a good trait but cannot feed bellies. You are a doctor. You have a bright future lying in front of you. Only a boy like Nikunj is suitable for you."

"Papa, Rahul is a hard-working boy. He is well educated and he is doing pretty well in his field. I don't know what Nikunj has told you. But trust me, Papa, Rahul is doing really well. He is an entrepreneur and has started his own manufacturing firm. He is a self-made person just like you. He is way better than that arrogant and insecure Nikunj."

Aditi was furious with Nikunj and in her entreaties with her father she could not refrain herself from voicing her resentment towards him as well; though she knew very well that her father would disapprove of this as he held Nikunj in high regard. Luckily for her, Rajender did not pay heed to Aditi's acrid comments. His attention was rather caught by what Aditi said about Rahul.

"A manufacturing firm! Manufactures what? Is it his own?" Finally, the man was coming around.

Aditi sighed in relief and explained Rahul's new venture in detail to her father. She assured her father that she and Rahul were very serious about their careers. While Rahul was working hard in his business, she herself was preparing for the PG medical entrance examinations. Aditi's father was finally convinced and admired his daughter's maturity. He asked Aditi to invite Rahul for dinner in the coming week. Aditi was overjoyed. She hugged her dad and went back to the hostel. She messaged Rahul and asked him to pick her up in the morning as she had a big surprise for him.

****

Aditi could not wait for the next day to dawn. Their early morning escapades had become common now. As she spotted his bike, she rushed down the steps of her hostel. She gave him a quick peck and sat behind him. Aditi's blatant display of love took Rahul not only by surprise but also fanned his desires for her more. She blushed at the way he looked at her; his eyes burning with desire for her. They stopped at the Ridge and Aditi told him about her conversation with her father the previous night. Rahul listened to everything with bated breath. Aditi finally told him about the invitation for dinner. Rahul was happy but looked so nervous at the thought of meeting Aditi's family that she could not control her laughter. Rahul was about to hug her when she ran away from there into the wilderness. Rahul chased after her and got hold of her hand as he caught up with her. As they looked at each other, they could see the yearning in their eyes.

Rahul stepped closer to her. Aditi clung on to his shoulder as his head bent low. Rahul, as he reached for her luscious lips, could smell a faint Shalimar fragrance emanating from her, maddening him, and making her even more irresistible to him now. His lips were on hers. The soft and velvety touch sent a strange shiver down his body. Aditi closed her eyes while Rahul's gaze went all over the face that he used to revere only from afar till now. And his hands involuntarily reached for the deepest curve on her back, pulling her closer against himself. Aditi's left hand travelled from his shoulder to his thick and soft mane and her fingers ran through them as their lips tasted each other hungrily. They were devouring each other like two amorous birds of prey. The chirrup of birds in the nearby thicket was the only sound they could hear besides their own panting. Rahul's hands were eagerly gliding over her curves. Hers had undone a few buttons over his shirt. The soft hands of Aditi were rubbing over his chest hair. This fomented his yearning to have her right there and then. His two hands clasped her firmly by her pelvis and slid up into her T-shirt, fondling her satin skin and undulating curves. Aditi was breathless as Rahul's lips were gliding down her neck by now. She could feel his warm breath over her bare skin. A strange sensation gripped her. Rahul had taken hold of her completely. His strong and muscular arms had wrapped her in a tight hold; not that she wanted to break free. She wanted to melt into him. But no amount of effort could seem to satiate their thirst for getting enough of each other. Rahul advanced forward holding her in her arms until her back leaned against a tree trunk. Rahul was bent over her, exploring her even more vigorously. The craving in her for him was no less. Just then they both heard the sound of approaching footsteps. They quickly adjusted their clothes and sat on a nearby rock. A man walked past them swinging a piece of a branch in circles and whistling to himself.

When he was sufficiently out of sight, Rahul and Aditi looked at each other and laughed. Rahul took her hand in his and locked his fingers in hers.

"I love you," he said, lifting their locked hands up and planting a kiss on the back of her hand while looking intently in her eyes.

It melted Aditi to see such passionate love in Rahul's eyes for her. She bent forward and kissed him on the corner of his mouth. In her smile Rahul found the reciprocation of his feelings. They sat there for some time breathing in the soothing wind blowing through the trees, listening to the bird calls, and soaking in the warmth of each other's love.

Finally, Aditi got hold of her emotions and told Rahul that since Diwali was round the corner, he could join them for dinner then. Rahul was still too moved to say anything. He let out an incredulous gasp. "Whatever you say, my dear." Both of them looked at each other. They saw the same dream in each other's eyes.

Aditi was worried about her career. She wanted to pursue MD in Paediatrics but the pandemic thwarted all her plans. The long duty hours didn't leave her with much time to study. On the other hand, Rahul got busy with the work in his new firm. It was a profitable business venture and the returns were quick and ample. The lifestyle of Rahul and Arun also changed considerably. Though work was enormous, the profits set them in a comfortable economic position.

Rahul and Arun soon bought a new car, a Creta, on Diwali. This was to aid them in their business which required them to travel around meeting new clients. It was an emotional moment for them. This was a purchase that they made with their own hard-earned money. Rahul also went on a shopping spree to buy good clothes to wear on the D-day.

In the evening, Rahul went to Aditi's house in his new car. Aditi had been waiting anxiously for him. Even though they had been together at the Hyundai showroom just a few hours back, she couldn't wait to introduce Rahul to her parents. Aditi's father was impressed by Rahul's mellowness, wisdom and sharpness of intellect. After speaking to Rahul, Aditi's father realised that his entrepreneurial trajectory was a result of extreme hard work, dedication and devotion. He found an extremely balanced and self-confident man in Rahul. Aditi was happy to see Rahul bond with her father. Later, she asked for her father's permission to go for a drive with Rahul, Anjali and Arun to celebrate the success of the boys. It was an ecstatic moment for them. All four of them went on a long drive in their new car. They drove through the Delhi roads for hours at night. The music was loud and the cold night air was blowing through Aditi's hair as she was peeping out of the car's window. They were swaying and singing. That night, the city sky reverberated with the laughter of friends, songs of lovers, and the joyous cries of an unprecedented success.

❑

10

CHAPTER

Jabbed for Life

"...and here you are living despite it all."

—Rupi Kaur

December 2020

The awful year finally reached its end. It was December and people across the world were hoping that as the year ended their woes would end too. They thought that maybe the year was jinxed and the new year would bring life back to normalcy as they had always known it. Their conjectures were not unfounded either. The cases dropped to an all-time low by the end of the year. India, at last, heaved a sigh of relief.

Aditi's workload in the hospital decreased considerably. The footfall was low. She could now resume her study for the PG exam which was barely few months away. Aditi had to give it her best shot. She had to make up for the lost time too. Therefore, she became terribly busy with her studies.

Rahul's firm on the other hand was giving exponential returns. He was getting a lot of orders from offices, local pharmacies and clinics. Balvinder was content to see that the investment that he made in the new firm proved to be fruitious. At his age and in his fragile health condition, nothing could be more desirable than getting a regular flow of income sitting at home. So, he was usually cheerful these days.

On the eve of New Year's Day, he was checking the accounts that Rahul had brought to him at his house. After inspecting them, he looked up at Rahul and asked him in a jolly way,

"So my boy, what's the plan for the day?"

"Well, after this I will go to the Care Clinic, the one owned by Mr Anoop. We got a call from them last week. So the plan is to get the deal through." Rahul spoke in a matter-of-fact way.

"Oh... leave that aside. All work and no play makes Jack a dull boy. Do not make yourself a dull boy. It's 31 December! Go and make merry." Balvinder was his usual playful and joyous self.

Only then did Rahul realise that it was the last day of the year indeed. A time to celebrate. He left Balvinder's house with a spring in his steps. As he sat inside the car, he started planning for the night. He wanted the last day of the year to be a special one for them. As the corona cases were on a declining trend and preparation for vaccinations were in place, he was pretty hopeful that things would soon return to normal. The government had put special restrictions for 31 December and the first week of January 2021 to avoid social gatherings in public places, bars and restaurants, etc. to prevent the spread of the virus.

Rahul had already started dreaming of building a life with Aditi. He decided to celebrate the last day of the most dreadful year with the love of his life. He called up Arun and let him in on his thoughts. Arun immediately set to work. He called up Anjali and asked her to connect with Aditi and make her come over to the Tulip hostel for the New Year celebrations.

Aditi had been expecting to celebrate the day with Rahul. But Anjali told her that Rahul and Arun had been called for an important meeting with a client and they wouldn't be able to join the celebration. Aditi was crestfallen but decided to join Anjali just to take her mind off Rahul. She couldn't bear to spend the last day of the year all by herself.

At night, as Aditi knocked at the door of Tulip hostel, Rahul opened the door for her. She was astounded and couldn't believe her eyes. All her anger vanished in that moment as she hugged him tight. Rahul stood there stupefied. Aditi was wearing a sequined golden dress with a fur overcoat thrown over it. She was every bit a diva. Rahul quickly composed himself and told her that the surprises had just begun.

Rahul blindfolded her and led her to the rooftop. She kept on asking him about his plan but he just told her to be patient and trust him. While she was climbing the stairs, a distinct aroma of jasmine emanating from the reed diffuser suddenly enveloped her and she could feel a cool air lightly embracing her. The romantic music playing in the background engulfed her senses completely. She was getting excited with each step she took and just then they reached the landing of the stairs.

When Rahul removed her blindfold, she couldn't believe her eyes. All the way from the door to the table in the centre of the roof, candles lit the path. As she walked on, she noted the surroundings further. The table had fresh pink and white rose petals spread over it and a very sleek and elegant vase holding a single red rose. A beautiful lamp was burning, creating shadows on the parapet. Heart shaped balloons were scattered on the floor. Aditi had never in her wildest dreams imagined Rahul to be so romantic. She looked at him and was completely smitten by the raw masculine charm he exuded. She wanted to kiss the stubble on his face that he had trimmed with extreme care, for he knew that Aditi loved it.

It was better than partying all night long at the so-called most happening party spots in Delhi. Just then, Arun and Anjali joined them. Aditi pretended to be angry with Anjali for siding with the boys but gave her a bear hug at the same time. Rahul poured white wine for all four of them. His traditional upbringing would have never allowed him to enjoy alcohol till a few months back. But frequent meetings with the clients, the stress of staying away from the family, Balvinder's health scare, the self-created pressure to make a niche for himself in Delhi and the company of friends like Manjeet had taught him how to enjoy drinks socially. Anjali had ordered vegetable kebabs and honey-chilli potatoes for starters. They were enjoying the chilly winter air with wine glasses in their hands and good food on the table.

All four were thankful for the evening in the proximity of their best friends. It was a breather for them after months of tumultuous working hours. They raised a toast to the good time they were having and felt blessed to have each other. Aditi suddenly got up and turned on the volume of the

Bluetooth speaker. She started swaying to the Punjabi party songs she had put on and made a reluctant Rahul dance with her. Arun and Anjali too joined them on the floor. Rahul was very concerned about the loud party music but Aditi had always lived in the moment. She had never worried about what any random person thought or believed. The way her body moved, and her hair flowed around her face, Rahul quickly overcame his shyness and started swaying to the music. As they were dancing, Rahul's hand slipped to Aditi's waist and pulled her closer to himself. He held her tightly in his embrace. His deep intense eyes were looking into her eyes. Aditi felt an irresistible push. His head tilted and he kissed Aditi on the lips. They were swaying slowly to the music holding each other in their embrace. None of them could think that the last hours of the year that wreaked havoc across the world would turn out to be so beautiful for them. Arun and Anjali wanted to steal some quiet moments together and so they excused themselves and retired to the quarters downstairs.

Rahul and Aditi were left alone on the terrace. The night had far advanced and both of them were inebriated. The conversation soon gave way to an impatient silence in which both were looking at each other with a desire never felt before. Rahul leaned forward and placed his lips on hers. It felt cold and gentle as was the Delhi winter air. Aditi closed her eyes. Her hands moved halfway to stop him but lost the resolve to do so as the kiss felt amazing. They kissed till she felt him shiver and groan. He looked into her eyes with affection and whispered "I love you baby". The stars twinkled above them. It was a magical night, a night to remember!

****

January 2021

The year 2021 began on a promising note. The pandemic was well under control. The city was again bubbling with activity. The next two-three months were a relief after a long tussle with COVID. Rahul and Arun were back to business. Rahul had impressively transitioned from being a job seeker to a job creator. He was working relentlessly on getting more and more orders for the firm. So, he oscillated from every nook and corner to seek orders and learn technicalities needed for any new avenue. He was working hard. This was his predominant trait which everyone was convinced of. But now Aditi was his reason for putting in so much hard work. He had to establish himself to be worthy of her.

Successful people are not gifted, they just strive for it. Rahul was one of that kind. It was not that Rahul and Arun did not face any difficulty in their new business, but whenever they faced any barriers and obstacles, they discussed them with Balvinder Singh who guided them in all respects. The never-ceasing urge to learn and grow is one of the key requirements for any budding entrepreneur. Rahul possessed it and was learning the modalities of this new business.

It was the first week of January; the weather was cold. Rahul had just finished his pending office work. It was 6 o'clock in the evening. The sky was clear, and the cold winter breeze was blowing. The lanes were enveloped in the darkness of the night. The market was bustling with people. Driving his car through the crowded market he reached home, unlocked the door, and entered the room. Today, he was more tired than usual. As soon as he lay on the bed, he fell asleep.

When his phone rang, he was in deep sleep. He was jolted from his slumber only when the phone rang for the third time. He picked the phone rubbing his eyes, but it got disconnected by then. The call was from home. He called back immediately.

Baba picked up. He asked, "Beta, is everything fine? No call from you for over a fortnight. We were worried about you."

"Nothing Baba, it's just work. There is a lot of work in the new start-up. So I was quite busy of late, and did not get time to call. Sorry, Baba. How is everyone at home?"

Baba replied, "Everyone is fine. Your Amma was worried about you, Son. You know her, how she makes a fuss when you do not call. But now she would be relieved. Get some rest."

Rahul hung the phone up. He had quite forgotten his family for a while amidst the fast pace of this city life. He felt a sense of guilt deep within. But it made his resolve to work and earn money even stronger. The faces of Amma, Baba, and his brother and sisters were revolving in his head. It was for all of them that he was working so hard, living away from his home.

****

John F Kennedy once said, "When written in Chinese, the word 'crisis' is composed of two characters—one represents danger, and the other represents opportunity." Kennedy's statement tells a deeper truth that crises can provide many opportunities and those who miss this might just be swept away by the economic and political storms the pandemic has unleashed.

The pandemic had made India realise that it should not be totally dependent on other countries for its needs. The national focus shifted from procurement to production. India emerged as a top generic drugs and vaccine manufacturer on the world scene. When the vaccination programme was rolled out, it was a giant leap. In the war against the pandemic, vaccination was the most reliable weapon available to any country. India came out with its home-grown vaccine called Covaxin, which was developed by Bharat Biotech in collaboration with ICMR and National Institute of Virology. While the Pune-based Serum Institute of India Ltd. (SII) had partnered with AstraZeneca to bring out the Oxford vaccine under the name 'Covishield'. This was another vaccine that India started its mass vaccination programme with.

The vaccination campaign thus began. The DMs and SDMs of all districts were entrusted with careful implementation of the same. The doctors were provided training before the first phase of the campaign.

Dr Ehsan had faith in Dr Aditi with whom he had earlier organised a blood donation camp successfully. He knew she would be apt for leading the training program in coordination with the District Immunization Officer. She was promptly enrolled for this, by Dr Ehsan. Dr Aditi first had to undergo a training programme in City Hospital at the behest of Dr Ehsan.

Doctors were trained to work with the newly launched CoWIN app for this purpose. CoWIN was an application where the list of people registered for vaccination was uploaded. Dr Aditi got the responsibility to train other officers too for this drive. She was soon appointed as the head of the trainer team. Her team trained the medical staff to deal with any complications arising during the vaccination process. The minutest details were taken care of like deciding on keeping the vaccinated person under observation for half an hour in a waiting room post-vaccination and how to follow up.

In the next phase of this training, civil defence volunteers were trained to handle the people going to be vaccinated. They were told about the safety guidelines regarding vaccination like maintenance of proper social distance, ensuring that people wore masks, proper sanitisation, thermal checking and maintenance of proper queues. Moreover, if they found any symptoms of COVID, they had to isolate such cases quickly and send them for the Rapid Antigen Test.

When the vaccination drive kicked off, the healthcare workers and frontline workers were the first to be vaccinated. As a result, Aditi received her first jab in the hospital. It was a proud moment for her and Aditi sealed it by clicking her selfie at the vaccination selfie point erected in the hospital. In no time, Aditi shared it with Rahul. Rahul felt relieved that now he would have to worry less for Aditi's safety in the hospital. As for him, that smile on her face was his vaccination.

The battle against the contagion thus began with full force as the vaccination programme was launched. Dr Ehsan's workload had never ebbed in these trying times. In the process he was always motivated by Ekta Yadav, his DM. He was the wheel that needed to keep turning for the world around him to remain in order. His day would start with visits to the vaccination centres to keep a close watch on the proper functioning of the drive. In case any adverse news from any centre was received, he took immediate action to resolve it. He had instructed his team, including the executive magistrates and the Nodal officers, to motivate their staff to cooperate with the people and facilitate them as far as possible. He and his team were ever ready for any challenge. His team was a motley of officials from various departments of the Delhi government. They were always present at the beck and call of Dr Ehsan. This crisis had brought all these officials together at one place and they felt as if they had found their true calling in the special task on which they were deployed. The way they could render their services to the people here was unsurpassable. Among them all, the notables were Parveen, Joginder and Sushil.

But these were strange times, whenever things appeared to be in order, something or the other would come up and create a stir. Hardly had the vaccination programme begun that rumours regarding COVID-19 vaccination spread in the society by the anti-vaxxers. This developed hesitancy towards vaccine among the people. Top google searches during the period went like these—

- Can a COVID-19 vaccine make me sick with coronavirus?
- Will the vaccine alter the DNA?
- Is the hurriedly developed vaccine really safe?

- Can vaccines cause infertility?
- Does the vaccine contain foetal tissue?

Many more rumours like these were doing the rounds. Dr Ehsan found himself in a fix on how to encourage people to get themselves jabbed. He discussed it with Dr Aditi. She was quick to suggest that they could take Rahul's help and make short videos that would bust such myths about vaccines. Dr Ehsan gave a nod to the idea. In the following days, Aditi and Rahul made videos that created awareness about the vaccines. Rahul provided the technical assistance and Aditi was the face of the videos. Manjeet recorded the videos. They created a YouTube channel for putting up all the content. Dr Ehsan uploaded all these videos on his sub-division's official portal also. It was an instant hit and became popular with RWAs. The videos soon garnered thousands of views.

"It's Aditi's magic. She has made the channel a smashing hit," Manjeet remarked. Rahul was intently looking at his laptop, engrossed in uploading their latest video.

"Right, bro!" Arun concurred with Manjeet as he stretched himself out on the sofa, tired from the day's work.

Aditi walked up to Rahul and ruffled his hair affectionately,

"No, it's because of Rahul." She smiled at him as he leaned back in the chair and looked at her.

"You seem to have a Midas touch, you know! Everything you touch turns into gold." Aditi winked at Rahul.

❑

11

CHAPTER

Chronicles of Agony and Pain

Grief is a very long journey,
A journey you take on your own.
And no one can know all the sorrow you feel,
For it is your sorrow alone.

—Anne Peterson

The vaccination programme took off in fits and starts. It was characterised by hesitancy among people in the beginning to a spurt towards the end of March. March was eerily different from the first two months of the year because the deadly head of the contagion was again rising up around the fag end of the month. Aditi's vaccination selfie still adorned Rahul's smartphone. Her beautiful smile, now fixed there on his phone's wallpaper, helped him sail through the most trying of times. Every day, when he woke and picked his phone up first thing in the morning, he would look at that dazzling smile and kiss it back.

Did the rising cases in the month of March ruffle any feathers? Not in the beginning. The already emboldened people in Delhi were quite hardy. They took it as yet another surge in the cases that would soon die down. The way earlier waves of the contagion in Delhi had left them largely unharmed, they were now mostly intrepid in their disposition.

Rahul's new venture did not leave him much time for himself or Aditi. Orders were coming in aplenty. Rahul and Arun were working like a Trojan at it. Whereas on the one hand Rahul's new venture was picking up steam, on the other side the contagion had surreptitiously sneaked in and was ready to strike with all its might.

Aditi too had her hands full with the vaccination drive and hospital work going on simultaneously. Assuagement in the last two months was giving way to a resurrection. Aditi was not unaware of this impending recurrence of the infection. She was on a round at a vaccination site when Dr Ehsan called her. It was an urge to expedite the vaccination process so that more people could be jabbed at the earliest.

"Doctor, we need to hasten this up. You see how cases are rising everywhere. Soon the situation may spiral out of control." Aditi sensed urgency in Dr Ehsan's voice. She had anticipated it. Only yesterday, she herself was reading an article in *The Lancet*. The threat was real and imminent. Her thoughts were occupied with Rahul who was still not vaccinated. She felt helpless and this irritated her even more. She remembered how, as a little girl, she said she wanted to be a doctor when she saw her grandmother dying from cancer in front of her eyes. She always thought that doctors have all the answers and all the power to save lives. And yet here, she sat defeated and clueless. She was even more vexed now as she saw the vaccine hesitancy in people and their complete disregard of COVID protocol. What else could she do? She sat there powerless.

****

April is the cruelest month...

The daily reporting of new cases which were in three figures till March soon rose to four in the month of April. The clouds of COVID were again hovering over the Delhi sky. But people had thrown caution to the wind. Within a matter of days, the cases rose dangerously. The numbers were baffling.

Ten days into the month, Delhi saw its second highest spike since the beginning of the pandemic. The hospitals were under a lot of pressure as the patients were turning up in increasing numbers. All of this happened so suddenly that people could not even comprehend the enormity of the catastrophe that had struck them. Aditi was busier than ever now. The demand for sanitisers and masks was rising again as the infection raised its hood higher and higher. There was an exigency for PPE kits.

Aditi's acquaintance, Mr Bajaj, who ran a private hospital in the city, was looking for a supplier of PPE kits and sanitisers. She wanted Rahul to grab this order. She knew that an order of this magnitude would turn the fortunes of Rahul's firm. For this, she talked to Mr Bajaj and told him about Rahul's manufacturing unit. Mr Bajaj in turn asked Aditi to arrange a meeting with Rahul.

Aditi called Rahul many times since morning but Rahul could not be reached. While Aditi was miffed at this, the increasing workload at the hospital was getting on her nerves too. Rahul was busy in a prolonged meeting with Balvinder over their firm's accounts. The work had increased greatly, and this left Rahul with little time. When he was finally free, he called Aditi back.

“Hey Aditi. I was really busy in a meeting with Mr Balvinder this morning. Sorry, I couldn’t take your call.” Rahul began on a note of apology.

“That’s okay, Rahul. I have a really big order for you to grab.” Aditi sounded rather cold. It was not just the fatigue from work but somewhere the incessant workload coupled with their high ambitions had created a rift between the two. Aditi gave Rahul Mr Bajaj’s details. “Rahul, don’t let this one slip. It will stand you in good stead in the market.”

“Rest assured. I will not leave any stone unturned,” Rahul said in an equally matter-of-fact way. It hurt Rahul whenever Aditi focused more on his business during their conversations as if his own being apart from his professional identity had no value for her. Aditi on the other hand, expected Rahul to be more proactive in the expression of his love for her. The conversation ended there as if that was all there was to say between the two.

****

The virus brought the entire system crashing to its knees within a matter of a few days. The unimaginable was happening again. And this time no one was being spared. The new variant was wreaking havoc on the people indiscriminately. While it was not clear as to how transmissible and dangerous the new Delta variant or B 1.617.2, a variant of SARS CoV-2 was, the effects of the second wave looked dramatically different from the first. This one came down with harsh severity. The long election schedules, pilgrimages, large rallies, and marriage functions across the country became super-spreaders.

The speed at which the virus was wiping out the population was of a different order. Its ability to infect even those who had taken adequate precautions, its lack of discrimination between the old, the young and the healthy, and the immunocompromised, vaccinated, or non-vaccinated, the unpredictability of its trajectory, and the increased number of deaths it seemed to be causing was of a horrifying magnitude.

The TV channels were abuzz with the frightening reports. Rahul was quite disturbed and called Baba to inquire if everything was all right over there. He instructed him to try not to go out of the house unnecessarily and remain in isolation in the house for as long as possible. Then he counselled him to get the necessary things delivered at home itself, and also advised him to be vigilant and get the first dose of vaccine at the earliest. Rahul blurted out everything in one breath. Baba could make out how anxious he was and assured him in return that they would take all the precautions.

He kept the phone down and realised that Goyal House was unusually silent and there was a quietude never experienced before. The loquacity of the place was missing. Rahul asked Hari Bhaiya to prepare a kadak ginger tea for him. Arun also joined him by then.

“Things will be very demanding from now on. It’s a crucial phase for our business.” Arun said, taking a seat beside Rahul.

“I know there is cut-throat competition,” Rahul concurred.

Arun knew that Rahul was giving all he had to this business and all that hard work was taking a toll on him.

"Rahul, you don't seem to be alright. You are looking very tired and gloomy," enquired a concerned Arun.

"Yes, Arun, I am worried as to how everyone will manage back home. The new wave isn't sparing anyone. Though I have discussed safety measures with Baba, the concern for their safety is leaving me distressed," said a visibly perturbed Rahul. The ferocity of the second wave had made him uneasy and his thoughts were there with his family.

"I know. But they will be safe. Don't worry. The hinterland will not be so affected. Remember how the cases were concentrated in only the cities last time?" said Arun.

"Right. I just hope they remain safe. We should also be careful nowadays. Whenever we are out, we must safeguard ourselves." The anxiety over the second wave was not leaving Rahul, even though he tried to make himself more optimistic.

Arun showed Rahul the sales figures over the last fortnight to cheer him up a little. Rahul took the laptop from him. His fingers started moving on the keyboard and he showed Arun the projections which were quite promising. Rahul's eyes lit up as he did so. It was at this juncture that Rahul remembered Aditi's proposal. He turned to Arun and told him about it. Arun was excited at this opportunity.

They talked to Mr Bajaj and began preparing a presentation for the same. Since this could be a breakthrough order for them, they did not want to leave any stone unturned. They sat through many nights preparing a presentation for their meeting with Mr Bajaj. One day when they were working on their presentation, Arun suddenly put his hand over Rahul's shoulder. Rahul turned back from the laptop screen and looked inquiringly at Arun.

"I can sense that it's not going well between you two." Arun told Rahul gently.

Rahul took a deep breath and shook his head. "Nothing. It's fine. Let us work." Arun felt that something had snapped in their relationship and Rahul was not sharing it. Rahul himself did not know what it was. It was just that a certain coldness had crept in their behaviour towards each other. And though each one of them wanted to end it, no one was able to.

****

Professor Bhanu Pratap was at home for the last three days. Before that, when he came back from the university, he felt more tired than usual. Initially, he blamed it on the effort that he had put in while writing his latest article. He thought that those long hours of sitting in the library had worn him out. But on the second day, when he had a high fever, his wife Savita decided to go for a COVID test.

The two lived alone. Their only son, Manjeet lived in a hostel in Delhi. Bhanu Pratap was a professor of history at Kurukshetra University. At the age of fifty-eight, he was a prolific writer.

Professor Bhanu Pratap was lying in bed. The thermometer on the bedside table still showed the reading that he took ten minutes ago. He felt that the thermometer perhaps had some glitch as he did not feel so worn down, after all, as one would be with a body temperature of 103° F. His wife was worried for him, but the professor made light of her worries. “Don’t worry. I will be up and about in a day. This is just a normal fever.”

Savita was not convinced though. She was waiting for the report. The doctor who lived next door had prescribed some medicines when Savita explained her husband’s condition to him.

It was 2 o’clock at night. Bhanu Pratap was quite uneasy. He sat up in bed. Even though he was in the bed for the last two days, the fatigue was extreme. He felt like he had run a mile and was not able to catch his breath. His mouth went completely dry. He felt dehydrated though Savita had made him drink plenty of water throughout the day. His hand reached for the glass of water on the table. The effort was too taxing for him and in his delusional state he floundered, and the glass toppled.

The sound of glass falling on the floor reached Savita’s ears. She was too sleepy to get the hang of it instantly. Five minutes had elapsed by the time Savita roused herself from sleep. She walked towards the room where Bhanu Pratap was sleeping. As she opened the door and switched the light on, her eyes fell on the glass lying on the floor with water spilled around it. The bed was empty. She looked around and saw the washroom door open. She walked across to the washroom, and to her dismay Professor Bhanu Pratap was lying on the washroom floor.

****

Delhi was looking at the next lockdown. The curve was rising sharply. The government started putting curbs on the movement of people again. In the midst of it all, the

Goyal House boys found the next topic of their discussion. Everything crashed so fast that people did not even have the time to chew over it. COVID tests were a nightmare. Sometimes, the test report would come after the person had succumbed to the disease.

Over the next two to three days, the situation was dire. A weekend curfew was imposed in Delhi. The hospitals were witnessing an unprecedented rush. People were running helter-skelter for Remdesivir, Fabiflu, Oxygen cylinders and Oxygen concentrators. Remdesivir was the new life-saving drug which was disappearing fast from the market and Amphotericin B, a medicine used to treat mucormycosis was scarcely available. The black marketeers were hoarding it. Demand and supply has such an intricate relationship that when the former goes up, the latter goes down. Even the most common drugs such as Paracetamol, Meftal, Vitamin C, etc were to be found with great difficulty at pharmacy shops.

Rahul missed his previous life which at least had some semblance of predictability in it. Ever since he had stepped into this city, he was on a roller coaster ride. Now he felt he was completely unable to comprehend what the next day would bring. The scenario was changing at a blinding rate.

The next day, as the boys were discussing the news of rising cases of coronavirus, Manjeet's phone rang. He went out to attend the call as the connectivity was poor inside their flat. After he came back, he hastily started packing his bag. The tension in his actions was palpable. Rahul inquired,

"Manjeet, what happened?"

"Rahul, Papa is not well. Maa sounded very worried. I have to leave right away."

"Okay, let me drop you at the Inter state Bus Terminal Anand Vihar. Don't worry, everything will be fine." They quickly left in Rahul's car.

The situation of the country, at this time, was going from bad to worse. The active cases went up by 41 percent which was a huge cause of concern. The number of daily casualties increased. This spike was a jolt for the nation. Healthcare workers too were affected by the disease. Aditi had to spend sleepless nights. So was the case with other doctors, nurses and para medical staff. They were staying at the hospitals only.

In that darkest night of her life, Savita was arguing with the hospital staff. "Do you have some humanity or not? Where else would I take him in this condition?"

"Look madam, your husband has come out COVID-positive in the Rapid Antigen Test. We do not treat COVID cases here as it's a non-COVID hospital. Sorry we cannot help you. You have to take him to a dedicated COVID hospital only."

Savita had to face great difficulty in carrying her husband to the hospital in the middle of the night. She had to ask her neighbour, Mr Kaushik, to help her in carrying Bhanu Pratap to the car. Mr Kaushik drove their car as Savita did not know how to drive. And now after all that hassle the hospital was turning them away.

She was not in a position to drive around the town again in search of hospitals. All her arguments and cries fell on deaf ears. The hospital administration did not budge. Savita anxiously looked around to find an answer. Mr Kaushik was nowhere to be seen either. Her heart sank. She realised that Mr Kaushik must have sneaked out after knowing that the professor was COVID-positive. Her fingers were trembling on the phone as she was searching for Manjeet's number. His phone was out of reach. Her desperate fingers were searching for the numbers of a few other people who were close enough to be of some help at this hour. A student of Bhanu Pratap responded to the call.

Savita was sitting beside her husband who was lying unattended in the hospital compound. She was holding his hand so as to make him feel that someone was there to take care of him. But he was insensate. Whenever he would gain his senses for a brief period, he would start shaking as if gasping for air. And then he would relapse again. The boy, whom Savita had called, came running to her. He was the only one who could be reached out at that hour and without having any close relation or being related by blood, there he stood lending a helping hand. He managed to get the professor into the car. The next few hours saw a race for life on the roads as they drove from one hospital to another in search of a bed. Savita was sitting in the back seat holding her husband. Her anxious heart was thumping inside her chest and her eyes were filled with tears. Her lips were moving in an inaudible prayer for her husband who was sinking every moment, by her side.

Manjeet had got down from the bus. He quickly took an auto rickshaw to the hospital where he was told that his father was admitted. He reached the hospital and took quick strides to the ICU. In the corridor, he saw his mother sitting on a bench.

"Maa! Maa! How is Papa?" Manjeet was kneeling by Savita's side who sat silently with her head bent low. Manjeet put his hand on her shoulder and shook her. She sat there like a stone.

Just then, he heard someone calling his name from behind. Manjeet turned. Professor Bhanu Pratap's student was looking at him with tearful eyes. He shook his head from side to side.

Manjeet's bag dropped from his hand, and he sat down with a thud right there on the floor. Savita put her hand on his shoulder. Manjeet turned back and held his mother. At this, Savita broke down and for the first time wailed loudly. The two sat there in that corridor, holding each other and sobbing inconsolably.

****

As the tsunami of COVID-19 cases hit, an unprecedented situation was unfolding as no one had witnessed chaos at this level. Uncountable bodies had piled in the mortuaries; people were struggling to find space at funeral grounds for their loved ones as pyres were being built in makeshift crematoriums. There was an acute shortage of oxygen cylinders across the country, which was generating a public health nightmare. People were experiencing mistreatment and denial of justice, the trauma of which would remain etched in memories for decades to come. The human catastrophe painted a grim picture, where people were left to die, and families pleading with the hospital authorities to admit their relatives who were desperately ill. India was in the grip of a devastating second wave of the virus and cities were facing fresh lockdowns. By mid-April, the country was averaging more than 100,000 cases a day.

It was 5 o'clock in the evening, when Rahul returned from the office. Ever since he dropped Manjeet at the railway station in the morning, he had been thinking of calling him. But the busy work schedule did not allow him to think of anything else throughout the day. He finally made the call and asked Manjeet about the well-being of his father. For the next two minutes Rahul stood transfixed, holding his phone over his ear and not knowing what to say. Manjeet's enormous tragedy shook him completely.

Rahul and Arun hastily set out for Manjeet's house. After a drive of about four hours the two reached there. The night was darker than usual. A handful of people were present, and a mournful silence enveloped the house. Manjeet stood in a corner, the cold wall supporting him. His eyes were red with grief. As Rahul hugged him, he broke down and wept convulsively. Rahul and Arun stood by Manjeet through it and supported him as best as they could. Manjeet stayed back with his mother who was now both lonely as well as ill. After the last rites had been performed, Rahul and Arun returned to Delhi. As a precautionary measure, the Government had imposed restrictions on gatherings during cremation—a very limited number of individuals were allowed to be present.

****

On 19 April, the city reported its highest single-day spike of 24,462 cases despite a weekend curfew. India had been reeling from a deadly second wave since the start of April. The outbreak was not just a crisis for India but for everyone.

"The virus doesn't respect borders, or nationalities, or age, or sex or religion," said Dr Soumya Swaminathan, the

World Health Organisation's chief scientist. "And what's playing out in India now, unfortunately, has been played out in other countries."

The pandemic had revealed just how interconnected the world was. And if a country had extremely high levels of infection, then it was likely to spread to other countries as well.

The oxygen crisis came when coronavirus cases continued to surge. Delhi alone reported more than 20,000 new infections and 407 deaths in one day. The situation was overly critical. Outside hospitals, families of patients who could not find a bed were struggling to get hold of portable cylinders—sometimes standing in queues for up to 12 hours.

Ever since Rahul returned from Manjeet's house, he had felt a little unwell. But it was not so much as to be of any concern to him. What happened to Manjeet was a jolt for Rahul. He was now deeply worried for his own family. This wave was not sparing even those who lived in far-flung areas. Rahul kept a close eye on the corona situation in his hometown as well.

What happened with Manjeet's father and the afflictions of people around him made a deep impact on Rahul. He thought that in such perilous times, while humanity was in grave danger, it was incumbent upon him to serve those who had no help in sight. Rahul heard of a man from Mumbai who had sold his SUV to provide oxygen cylinders to people in need. He read about an auto rickshaw driver who had converted his auto into a mobile ambulance fitted with oxygen to help the people in need. Rahul could hardly spare any time during the day. So, he decided to provide help at night. He got in touch with a local gurudwara where free oxygen seva was being given. He worked there from 12–4 in the morning and helped people refill their oxygen cylinders on days when he could find time from his already hectic schedule.

The times were trying, and a tragedy of great degree was unfolding around him. Rahul took his phone out of his pocket and saw Aditi's photo again. Her beautiful smile that used to make him happy every time he saw it, had lost its magic, it seemed. For the first time, he felt an ache in his heart seeing her smile. Somehow, the photo and the smile in it had moved far back into a time when the world was a better place than this and people were more humane too.

Rahul was thus lost in thoughts when he got a call from Dr Ehsan. Rahul was a little perturbed to see a call at that hour. It was almost midnight.

"Hello, Rahul! There is a critical situation, and we need your help."

Dr Ehsan was talking about a five-year-old boy in the nearby area. The boy's father was a construction worker. It turned out that the boy was COVID-positive and in the scenario where Delhi was reeling under the second wave with hospitals sending out SOS calls for oxygen and even the most affluent of people were turned away from hospitals, the poor family had no hope. Dr Ehsan asked Rahul to take the boy to the hospital in his car while in the meantime, Dr Ehsan was trying to exercise his powers to secure a bed for the boy there. Time was crucial as was in Professor Bhanu Pratap's case. Rahul could not waste a second. He jumped out of bed and asked Arun to come along. Arun knew that Rahul had not been feeling well for the past few days. He asked him to take rest while he would go and handle everything on his own. Rahul was not one to balk at the situation.

The helpless father was standing outside his shanty. He folded his hands before Rahul and Arun when the two arrived there. They had got hold of an oxygen cylinder on their way from a vendor as directed by Dr Ehsan.

Rahul went inside the shanty. The mother was holding the boy in her lap. The boy had turned pale and was panting. The mother was fanning him with the edge of her sari. Arun followed behind. The woman saw them and started crying.

"Save my child! God will bless you, please save my child!" she pleaded.

"Don't worry. We are here now. He will be fine." Arun tried to comfort her and took the boy out of her arms.

Next, Arun was running with the boy in his arms towards the car. Rahul swiftly got behind the wheel and sped towards the hospital as Dr Ehsan had asked them to.

Rahul made a call to Dr Ehsan while driving the car as fast as he could.

"Sir, the boy is with us. We are going towards the hospital now."

"Good, Rahul. I have arranged a bed in the nearby Government hospital for him. You can go ahead. Brief me when you get him admitted."

Time was of utmost importance. The tiny body of the boy was struggling for oxygen. He was gasping and a wheezing sound came out of his lungs every time he made a vigorous attempt to breathe. Arun's heart was ready to burst at the sight of a small boy struggling for life.

"Faster, Rahul," Arun would scream fearing for the boy's life. The car was speeding on the road making its way through the sparse traffic towards the Government hospital. The oxygen cylinder was lying in the car but neither of the two knew how to use it.

Just as the car screeched to a halt in the hospital parking lot, Arun opened the car door without wasting a second and ran with the boy still in his arms. Rahul came running behind him with the oxygen cylinder. Dr Ehsan had made arrangements in the Government hospital and so the boy was immediately attended to. He was quickly put on oxygen and was taken to the ICU from there. No stretcher was available, and time could not be wasted on such trifles, therefore Arun carried him to the ICU in his arms with one person carrying the oxygen cylinder along. The boy got the bed and oxygen cylinder—the two things in Delhi that were near impossible to get hold of at that time.

But the bed and oxygen cylinder were not a guarantee of survival either. Where people were dropping dead like flies, Rahul had every reason to be afraid. He kept a close watch on the boy's condition over the next week. He left Arun to take care of the firm and spared him the field visits as Arun often complained about being fatigued. The boy's condition gradually improved, and finally he was out of danger. Rahul broke down into sobs when he heard this from the doctor after seven days of the boy's hospital stay. Wiping his tears off, he smiled at the doctor and said, "Thank you!"

That one week was emotionally overtaxing for Rahul. Though he was greatly relieved that they could become instrumental in saving the boy's life, yet the grim spectacle of battle for life in the hospitals was enough to break down even the strongest of people.

****

Mayhem in May

What followed in the coming days was something that nobody could ever expect. The onslaught of the pandemic in Delhi this time around was disastrous. Everyone knew someone who was infected. Those who were infected became seriously ill. If one member caught the infection, it spread quickly to others too. Soon, hospital beds became scarce. Patients were gasping for oxygen. All of this happened within a matter of days. It looked like the corona bomb was ticking all this while and the people had slackened in their complacency.

The grieving people were making frantic calls and posting appeals across social media platforms in a bid to save their loved ones. The virus made no distinction between the rich or the poor. The way it galloped through the city, it left everyone in the lurch, be they affluent or destitute. Dr Ehsan received incessant calls from all quarters. It was late at night when Dr Ehsan was finally relieved of his office duties for the day. He had just sat down to break his fast in the evening with the family. He was observing roza, and the iftar—an evening meal with the family—was something he held dear. Just then, he received a call from Rupali, a high-ranking IAS officer. She was very distressed and requested an oxygen cylinder for her father in Ghaziabad. She was puzzled as despite her die-hard efforts she was not able to arrange a cylinder for her father. She posted appeals on her social media accounts as well, but to no avail.

On her request, the COVID command team of Dr Ehsan's sub-division was activated. Since it was a distress call, it had to be resolved in time. Impressed by the way Rahul and Arun had handled the case of the five-year-old boy, Dr Ehsan entrusted them with this case as well.

Rahul and Arun went to the vendor they were told about. The vendor immediately backtracked and professed his inability to provide them with a cylinder. Rahul and Arun tried politely first but when he did not acquiesce, they knew how to be resourceful. With their sheer tactfulness, they were able to grab one oxygen cylinder from the vendor. Finally, they loaded the oxygen from Shalimar Bagh and delivered it to Rupali in Ghaziabad. A relieved Rupali thanked Rahul and Arun, two godsent angels. Rupali called up Dr Ehsan to convey her thanks.

It was quite late in the night when the two returned to Goyal House. Arun was exhausted by these charitable excursions and could not drive anymore, so Rahul took over and drove the car back. The city wore a doleful look. As their car was cruising on the road, it seemed as if the very air of Delhi was grieving. Their car passed by a crematorium; there was a grim race there as well. People were standing in large numbers outside, with the dead bodies, waiting for their turn. On the roads, the sirens of the ambulances were wailing. There was a macabre dance of death everywhere. It was enough to break anyone's spirit.

After returning, they took a bath and sanitised their belongings. Rahul saw that Arun was looking paler than usual. But Arun was dismissive of Rahul's apprehensions and said that he was just very tired. Arun went off to sleep. He refused to eat anything as he was very fatigued.

Rahul was sitting alone in the common room today. The sight of people jostling for life and of the dead jostling for cremation had disturbed him so much that he found it difficult to sleep. He switched the TV on and watched the sad spectacle of the onslaught of the virus there as well. It was disheartening. He turned it off. He was fidgeting with the things lying around as if something was ailing him from within. Like some unresolved issue that disturbs you all the time and does not let you rest for a while. Aditi came back to his mind. All his pretensions that there was nothing amiss between them were false. His heart knew that, but his mind was dismissive. The tussle went on and finally his heart got the better of him. He picked up his phone and tapped Aditi's name in the call list.

"Hey... are you okay?"

"Yeah... what happened? Where are you? Did you not have that meeting today with Mr Bajaj?"

"Oh yes, the meeting... it has been postponed."

"What? Why?"

"Something else came up suddenly. So I requested him to postpone the meeting."

"What! Are you crazy? You cannot take it so lightly. Do you realise how big this one order would be for you?"

"Aditi, I did not call to talk business."

There was a moment's silence after which Aditi spoke,

"Rahul, don't forget, business is important if we want a future for our relationship."

Aditi regretted it the moment she uttered these words. But the way Rahul had remained incommunicado for the past days and Nikunj was getting closer in her family's confidences, she had become restless. But before she could say anything to allay the damage her words might have caused, she heard Rahul saying,

"All right, Aditi. Next time I will call you only when there is a business deal to discuss. Bye."

Rahul did not mean to discuss meeting or work with Aditi. But Aditi's business-like tone and cold approach prompted Rahul to withdraw. He felt that all that he had wanted to say was knotted up in his throat. He yearned to hear that tender voice of Aditi again. Where was it lost? Aditi seemed to have changed greatly. She was becoming colder and distant. Rahul could not bring himself to talk any further. Rahul felt alone, very alone in that room. He lay back on the couch and dozed off.

Aditi was not indifferent. But the city was. The city, where people were dying without oxygen, was stony and cold. Aditi was a witness to the spectacle of death every hour of the day in that dreary hospital ward. Aditi loved Rahul but the time and place was not favourable for any tenderness and care to spring up and flourish.

Aditi's face flushed and she leaned against the wall. The beep sound after Rahul unceremoniously hung the phone was still ringing in her ears. Her eyes welled up at the harsh words that Rahul had just spoken for the first time while talking to her. Dr Nikunj, who was on round duty in the ward saw Aditi standing like that, dejected and leaning on the wall. He quickly approached her and was aghast when he saw her tearful eyes. Never had he seen Aditi looking so broken and weak.

"Aditi!"

Aditi looked towards Nikunj, and the tears fell down her cheeks. She quickly tried to wipe them with the back of her hand, adjusting her double layered face mask.

"What happened? Are you okay?"

Aditi took a deep breath and tried to brush it away, but she was in such agony that she failed to do so. Tears welled up afresh in her eyes.

"Come on, Aditi, I know you have been mad at me of late. But you can still share with me what is bothering you."

Dr Nikunj's tender words touched her heart. Above all, she wanted to share this intense emotional burden that was too heavy for her to bear anymore.

"Nikunj, you know Rahul just spoke in such a harsh manner..." Aditi's head bent down, she took a deep sigh, and could not speak further.

Dr Nikunj felt angry with Rahul's behaviour.

"How dare he treat you like that? He should be grateful that a girl like you loves him. Otherwise, what is he in front of you? I mean he is just a small-town boy. Look at his audaciousness!" All the bitterness in Dr Nikunj's heart against Rahul found a way out in his words.

When those words fell on Aditi's ears, she became uncomfortable. It irked her a great deal hearing such words for Rahul.

"No, Nikunj. Please don't speak like that about Rahul."

"Aditi, I fail to understand you! There you are, so hurt by his behaviour just a moment ago and now unable to hear a single word against him. Aditi, I don't understand! What is it that draws you towards him?!"

Though Aditi was really hurt by the way her relationship was going with Rahul, through ups and downs, Nikunj's probing words kindled the tender emotions she held deep in her heart for Rahul just below her present feelings of anger and frustration at him.

"What draws me towards Rahul?" Aditi got lost in the image of Rahul that she had engraved there in her very consciousness, irrevocably.

"Yeah. Exactly. I mean what's so special about him?"

"What is there that does not draw me towards him? I can still remember that first day when I saw him in this very place. Yes, Nikunj, this is exactly where I saw him for the first time. Those deep eyes were looking at me. There was an air of nonchalance about him. And yet I saw him in a state of concern for someone with whom he had no relation. And I wondered if such men still existed, fighting tooth and nail for an unknown person!"

Dr Nikunj saw deep love in Aditi's eyes for Rahul. For the first time he realised how strong their love was for each other and thereby how futile his own attempt to win her over from Rahul.

"Nikunj, everything about him is special! The way he looks at me. It is different. No one has ever looked at me like that. I feel I am the most beautiful woman in this world when his eyes behold me. No one else could make me feel like that. When he talks to me, his attention is so riveted on me that I feel as if I am the most special person in this world for him. I feel protected when he is around me."

Aditi sighed and a smile spread across her face at the very thought of Rahul.

"Oh Nikunj, what is not there to like about him! He has a golden heart; kind and caring to everyone. How can I not love him? When he laughs, it feels like spring is in the air. When he cares for me, I melt in the warmth of that care. When he showers his love on me, it feels as if the first drops of monsoon are pouring down. Nikunj, every time I look at him, I fall in love with him all over again."

"Oh Aditi! I never knew you loved him so much! Please forgive the harsh words that I used against him. I am sorry. As a friend, I will only advise you not to bother about his harsh behaviour. The times are tough for all of us, and we all tend to lose our temper. You both will sail out of it. Trust me."

Aditi was relieved. Her own words had reinstated her faith in her love for Rahul. Additionally, Dr Nikunj's words gave her the comfort that she needed at this hour. Aditi could now understand what Rahul was feeling but she assured herself that everything would be all right after that ordeal was over.

Next morning, Rahul woke up from his slumber on the couch. The sun was high up in the sky and Goyal House was as silent as a grave. This was rather unusual. Just then Rahul remembered that Manjeet was not there. But what about Arun? Where was he? Rahul went to Arun's room and saw him still lying in the bed. This was rather surprising as Arun was not the one to stay in bed for long. A perturbed Rahul having an inkling of something amiss went near him and touched his forehead. It felt hot like a piece of burning coal. Rahul went cold and his heart sank. He shook Arun. But Arun was in delirium.

Rahul frantically called the only two people he could reach to in this hour of dire need. Dr. Ehsan quickly arranged for an RT PCR test for Arun. Aditi wrote down a few medicines for Arun and messaged the same to Rahul. For the next two days, Rahul took complete care of Arun. He cooked for Arun with his own hands and gave him medicines on time. Arun was mostly bedridden and ran high-grade fever along with cough for days.

Rahul had just given Arun a cup of tea when he checked that Arun's test report was finally available online. As he opened it, the worst of his fears came true. Arun came out positive. When Aditi found out about it, she asked Rahul to get himself tested too and maintain distance from Arun. Arun was now keeping a record of his temperature and oxygen levels. Rahul would keep calling on him from outside the room to make sure that he did.

Goyal House, that used to be filled with the laughter of boys, was desolate now. With Arun confined to his room, it became a grim place for Rahul. He worked from home most of the time so as not to leave the ailing Arun alone. In the next two days, Rahul's COVID test report also came out. It was negative. Rahul was doubtful about his own health in the past days. So apart from a COVID test, he went ahead with an antibody test also. Rahul's doubts were not unfounded. He had developed antibodies which meant that Rahul himself had become infected but remained asymptomatic.

Three more days had passed. Arun was still running a fever and his cough had exaggerated. Rahul was sitting out on the balcony sipping on a cup of coffee in the evening. Mr Bajaj's message flashed on the screen of his phone. He asked for a meeting in the next week. Rahul took no time in assenting to it. Rahul's joy knew no bounds and he thought of sharing the good news with Arun.

"Hey, guess what, we are going to have a meeting..." Rahul stopped abruptly. He was peeping into Arun's room with the door slightly ajar. Arun was lying on the bed gasping for breath in the same way as that five-year-old boy was gasping in Rahul's arm that night.

Rahul was driving towards City Hospital with Arun lying on the back seat. Aditi had arranged for a bed there. His hands were trembling on the steering wheel and his eyes were constantly shifting to the rear-view mirror. For the first time in the last one month, Rahul felt utterly scared.

❑

12
CHAPTER

Love Triumphs Over All

We make our own rainbows when we smile through our tears.

—Peggy Toney Horton

Rahul could hear distant loud wails all around. He tried to tune out all the noise but the persistent cries knocked him out of his deep sleep. He took a moment to absorb his surroundings. He was in the hospital's waiting area, where he had been staying ever since Arun was admitted to the hospital. A portentous terror seized him as he saw Kayansh's mother shrieking disconsolately. He went over to enquire what the matter was and Kayansh's father, who was as woebegone as his wife, informed Rahul that their son had just succumbed to a heart attack. Arun and Kayansh had been admitted to the hospital together, a week ago. They were on adjacent beds in the ICU. Arun had told Rahul about Kayansh's jovial nature and how he was able to make the others look beyond the dull and drab moments of the ICU to a wonderful future, free of the deadly pandemic. Kayansh's vitals were all fine until a few hours earlier. It was a shock even for the doctors when he suffered a major cardiac arrest and succumbed to it. All their efforts to revive him went in vain. Rahul was dumbstruck as he heard this. There was a blinding darkness all around him. He had a sinking feeling and he sat himself on a chair with great difficulty. Kayansh was barely twenty-five. Over the past one week, Rahul had developed a rapport with his family. They shared constant updates about each other's patients, became happy when there was any hope of a better treatment and shared the sorrow when any patient succumbed to the virus.

Rahul heard the ringing of a phone from a distance but took a minute to realise that it was his own phone. His unsteady shaky hands took the phone out of the pocket. The call was from Dr Ehsan, enquiring about Arun's health. As he told Dr Ehsan about Arun's grave condition, the pain in Rahul's voice was palpable. It distressed Dr Ehsan beyond measure but he had to put up a bold front for Rahul. Arun's strong, well-built frame flashed through his eyes. He had relied so many times on Arun and Rahul for their selfless services that it was difficult for him to visualise Arun struggling for life. Deep in his heart, Dr Ehsan hoped that Arun would take the phone from Rahul and tell him what he needed help with. He tried to reassure Rahul but he himself didn't trust the words coming out of his mouth. He had witnessed so many heart-rending scenes around him that he hoped against hope that Arun would survive this onslaught of the virus. The hospitals were overflowing with patients, the doctors were working beyond their human limits, and the life-saving drugs were in acute shortage. People were seeing their worst fears turning true. Dr Ehsan offered Rahul to approach him if any help was required from his side. As the vaccination drive for people in the 18+ age group had started recently, Dr Ehsan asked Rahul if he had been jabbed. Rahul had been juggling between taking care of Arun and managing the business and hardly had any time left for himself. He was unable to provide seva at the gurudwara langar either. He told Dr Ehsan that he'd been unable to get himself jabbed yet. Dr Ehsan was so exasperated at Rahul's apathy towards himself that he severely reprimanded him, just like an elder brother would. Rahul was rather touched and agreed to get himself vaccinated at the earliest.

As Rahul disconnected the call, he made a mental note to book a slot for his vaccination as soon as possible. He realised that he had to attend the meeting with Mr Bajaj in the afternoon. Even though he wanted to cancel the appointment with Mr Bajaj, he knew that everyone around him, especially Aditi and Balvinder Singh were expecting this opportunity to materialise. He dragged his feet to the exit gate but felt a little dizzy and not alert enough to drive over to Mr Bajaj's office himself. Rahul kept seeing Kayansh's face and found it difficult to get him out of his mind. He took a big gulp of water from his bottle and decided to book a cab instead. Before he left, he asked the nurse on duty if any medicines were required for Arun. She gave him the prescription.

He stopped at a pharmacy to purchase the medicines needed for Arun. While the pharmacist was taking out the medicines, Rahul's attention got riveted to a bunch of young kids performing acrobatics near a kirana store that was very crowded. They didn't accost anyone but Rahul could make out that they needed money as their joyful faces belied their deep miseries. They normally performed at the traffic lights, but because of the lockdown not many people were on the roads. Chemist shops and kirana stores, however, were always crowded. That became their working area. Rahul could see the pain in their eyes. They noticed Rahul looking in their direction and started performing for him exclusively. He offered them some money which they gladly took. He didn't want to make a spectacle in the market, but nonetheless he asked the kids why they were out on the streets when the government had imposed a strict lockdown.

The kids had a forlorn look about them. Most of them belonged to families of migrant labourers and as the government had announced complete lockdown, their parents had been left without any work. They had to come out in search of work, because if they didn't get any money, they would starve to death with their families.

There was a pair of twins in the group. They were barely six years old and their parents had succumbed to the illness a week back. The landlord had thrown them out of the house and they didn't have a place to live. They were living on the streets with other homeless people and were forced to beg for food. The tales of hunger and angst were writ large on their foreheads. Rahul felt queasy listening to their tales of agony. He couldn't bear to look them straight in the eyes. He remembered the same scenario which had played out last year when national lockdown was imposed for the first time. Several families had been affected by it and despite the government's best efforts, such daily wage earners had faced trials and tribulations beyond measure. And since this deadly second wave had wiped out many breadwinners, the situation was even grimmer this time around. Rahul was at a loss for words. He didn't know how to help those little faces who were struggling against all adversities with hope in their hearts and smiles on their faces. It was this spirit of childhood which made him believe that the world would soon tide over this crisis and Arun would be by his side again. Rahul gave them some money to get food for themselves. He gave them the number of one Mr Sushil from the COVID Command Team set up by the SDM office to help the people in need. Rahul gave them information about ration distribution centres set up by the government. The children were very happy at this stroke of luck. Their eyes gleamed with hope and they thanked Rahul Bhaiya profusely. They were hopeful that they would be able to satiate their hunger after all.

Rahul felt a sense of accomplishment. As he reached Mr Bajaj's office, he was bowled over by the magnificence of the office complex. He knew about the chain of hospitals owned by Mr Bajaj but didn't expect the office complex to be so formidable. He said a little prayer to the Almighty to strike the deal for him. As Rahul entered the office and introduced himself, the receptionist quickly spoke to the MD and asked Rahul to wait in the conference room. Mr Bajaj didn't take long to join him there. He was in his mid-fifties. A tall and muscular man, he had an aura of energy around him. His dense beard more than made up for his bald head. His pleasing personality and warm smile helped a nervous Rahul relax. Mr Bajaj was accompanied by his team. Arun and Rahul had worked very hard on the presentation and if he bagged the deal, he was sure that Arun would be very proud of him. He quickly set up his laptop and projected his presentation on the board. Though Rahul was very confident of his presentation and wanted to clinch the deal as early as possible, he understood the need to be patient and perceptive to the client's demands. His patience and hard work paid off and the presentation went very well. He specified the product details and the manufacturing process to Mr Bajaj and agreed to customise the products as per their requirements. He even produced a sample pack of the products so that Mr Bajaj could verify the quality himself.

Rahul's apt responses and the enthusiasm reminded Mr Bajaj of his own youth. Mr Bajaj had been apprehensive about giving such a big order to a young entrepreneur on Aditi's recommendation but was dazzled by Rahul's business acumen and appreciated his regard for details. Rahul was also impressed by Mr Bajaj's professional etiquette and straightforward nature. This mutual admiration ensured that they wanted to work in collaboration with each other at the earliest. Both were equally eager to strike a deal and it was decided that the delivery would be started from the next week itself.

Rahul left Mr Bajaj's office and immediately rushed back to the hospital. He was ecstatic about the deal and wanted to share the wonderful news with the two people of paramount value in his life, the ones who had stood by him through thick and thin—Arun and Aditi. He was yearning to thank Aditi for pushing him to attend the meeting. She was the Lady Luck whose power was shining on him and ensuring that his future was bright.

While coming back from Mr Bajaj's office, Rahul contemplated the reasons behind the drift in their relationship. He realised that he couldn't blame Aditi for the wrong turns in their relationship. Jealousy, insensitivity and distrust are not uninvited guests in a relationship. They enter each time a person feels ignored or uncared for and grow tentacles whenever a relationship is taken for granted. Rahul knew that he lacked the intensity and ferociousness of Aditi's love, but he had always depended upon his steadfastness and dedication towards her. Apparently, it was not sufficient. Rahul analysed that the fissures in their relationship were not because of Dr Nikunj but because of his own insecurities coupled with the nerve-racking toll taken by the pandemic. His possessiveness had made him lose sight of the beauty of their relationship and all he could think of was how to make up for the time that he had lost in his foolishness. He was thinking about all the tender moments that Aditi and he had spent together, and the way their eyes had always communicated with each other without uttering a word.

He straightaway went to the doctor's duty room to see if Aditi was there. Having contemplated over the distance in their relationship, he had realised his folly, and he couldn't waste even a minute away from Aditi. He wanted to tell her how much he loved her and how sorry he was to have wasted so much time because of his jealousy and foolishness. Since Aditi wasn't around, Rahul called her up. The phone kept ringing but there was no answer. The nurse in charge told him that Aditi had left for home and would be coming for the night shift at around 8 p.m. She also told him that Arun was stable and so he could relax at home and come back later to check on him.

Rahul desperately wanted to speak to Aditi but didn't want to do it over the phone. He kept pacing up and down in the waiting area for some time and then decided to catch forty winks at home and come back later when his 'Adu' was around. He couldn't let anything go wrong from here. He had to apologise for his silly childish behaviour and also take responsibility so that no negativity or misunderstanding could creep up between them, ever. He left the hospital instructing the nurse to update him if Arun's condition took a turn for better or for worse. The hospital staff knew him not just because of Aditi but also because of the selfless services he had offered during the pandemic. From arranging oxygen in critical times to providing Remdesivir and convalescent plasma with the help of the SDM office, he had proven to be a reliable and dependable person. The nurse happily obliged and asked him to relax.

****

It was 7:30 p.m. As he popped his head into the doctor's duty room searching for Aditi, he saw the nurse fumbling for something in the drawer. She anxiously went over to him and told him that Dr Aditi had come in early and was taking a round of the COVID ward and would be back any minute. Rahul sensed a little apprehensiveness in the nurse's voice but was so engrossed in his own thoughts that he missed it. He was wretched beyond imagination and only Aditi could help him out of his misery. Despite Aditi's requests of not hanging around in the doctor's room for fear of catching the even more infectious strain of the coronavirus, the delta plus virus, which was doing the rounds, Rahul decided to wait there only. He wanted to express his feelings to her at the earliest.

Aditi was back in twenty minutes but it seemed like eternity to Rahul. Aditi came back but she looked ruffled. He sensed something terribly wrong in her demeanour. He enquired about Arun's health and Aditi told him that the situation was worrisome. On the one hand they were left with only five hours of oxygen in the hospital, and on the other hand Arun needed convalescent plasma as the next line of treatment. Remdesivir was not helping with his symptoms. His oxygen levels were dipping and every breath he took was laboured. Kayansh's passing away had also deeply impacted his spirits. She advised Rahul to arrange for a backup cylinder for Arun as she wasn't sure if they would receive oxygen in time at the hospital despite having sent out an SOS for the same. Rahul took a minute to process what Aditi had just told him. He forgot all about his plans of proposing to Aditi and started thinking hard about what to do next. Aditi also told him that Arun was absolutely down in the dumps and if he lost hope, then even the best treatment would not work. Rahul was processing the implications of what Aditi had just said. He decided to call Anjali to the hospital. She could be with Arun to look after him while Aditi arranged for plasma and he somehow tried to get oxygen. Aditi was hesitant about allowing Anjali in the COVID ward but then Rahul talked her into it. She couldn't suggest any better option either. It was not in Aditi's hands to allow Anjali in proximity of a COVID patient in the hospital. She would have to seek approval from the Nodal in-charge. However, she told Rahul that she would arrange it all. His immediate task was to arrange an oxygen cylinder for Arun.

Rahul called up Anjali and told her about Arun's health. She was devastated. Never in her wildest dreams had she imagined that Arun's condition would deteriorate so much. She promptly agreed to Rahul's suggestion when Rahul told her that he would pick her up in half an hour's time. Anjali quickly dressed up in Arun's favourite suit, put on the little bindi that he loved on her face, downloaded his favourite music on her phone and took his favourite, The Alchemist. She didn't want him to feel desolate. While she was waiting for Rahul, she kept on thinking as to how she would perk up Arun's spirits. When the doorbell rang, she quickly picked her thoughts together and came out. Rahul had imagined Anjali in a desperate mood, but one look at her determined eyes made him realise how adversity emboldens people. He was glad to see a resolute Anjali ready to challenge the virus that bogged down the spirits of her boyfriend. Wearing their face masks, both approached the City hospital.

Rahul dropped her at the hospital and then set off for the gurudwara where he did seva earlier. He was pretty hopeful that he would be able to arrange a cylinder from there. But he was crestfallen when they told him that they had supplied all the oxygen cylinders to a nearby nursing home which was left with just an hour-long oxygen supply for its patients. Now they only had a few empty cylinders with them. Rahul had pinned his hopes on managing a cylinder from there. He couldn't think of any other alternative. He had already called up Dr Ehsan who had been receiving SOS calls from many hospitals in his jurisdiction for supply of oxygen. He had posted on his Facebook page regarding the same but was aghast at people's responses. There were so many numbers passed on to him by known people, but none of them was working. Some numbers were switched off while some other numbers that answered didn't have any knowledge of oxygen availability, and a few others were out of oxygen cylinders. He wanted to blast the people who were busy forwarding numbers from one group to the other without verifying their authenticity. He felt that all his selfless work till date had been futile. Now when he needed help for his friend, there was no one he could count upon. He felt let down by the blessings and good wishes of all the people he had helped in the pandemic. He had always maintained his calm and balance even in the most adverse of situations but now when it was about Arun, he just couldn't keep his head together. He needed to find a way. He looked up at the sky as if hoping for some divine intervention. His phone buzzed. It was Manjeet. He had received the information that an oxygen plant in Manesar was refilling the oxygen cylinders for patients. One had to take the RT PCR report of the patient along with the Aadhar card to get the cylinder filled. Though there was a 2–3-hour-long queue there, it was for sure that one would get oxygen. But an empty oxygen cylinder was needed for it. Rahul told Manjeet that he would immediately arrange an empty cylinder from the gurudwara. Manjeet sprang into action on hearing this. He advised Rahul to go back to the hospital and be with Arun; meanwhile he would go and get the oxygen cylinder re-filled from Manesar only, if nothing else worked out. Rahul heaved a sigh of relief. He would now be able to see if Aditi had managed to get convalescent plasma for Arun or if anything else was required.

He made his way back to the hospital. Aditi was in the doctors' duty room. She had spoken to Dr Ehsan regarding convalescent plasma. She had tried several contacts earlier but to no avail. Then she remembered the initiative launched by Dr Ehsan where they had made a database of people eligible as well as willing to donate plasma after recovery from COVID disease. She had received a few matching donors and was now trying to get in touch with them. Rahul asked her how Arun was doing. She was concerned about Arun's fluctuating SpO2 levels and the COVID pneumonia that he had developed. His HRCT score was 19 and his D-dimer and CRP levels were also very high. Arun's condition was completely unpredictable. As a doctor, she had seen many patients recover even after having higher values than Arun. But the heart always fears the worst for the loved ones. Rahul could look straight through her. He had always had this ability to read what was going on inside her mind. He saw fear in her eyes as she worded her thoughts, "The next few days are crucial for him. He has to be constantly monitored. If he sails past this, then we can be pretty hopeful about his recovery. He needs all the physical and emotional strength to fight the disease."

Rahul took the list of plasma donors' numbers from Aditi and started to help her out by calling the remaining people. An hour down the line and more than 30–35 calls later, they were beginning to lose hope as nothing had worked out. They looked at each other, aghast, their eyes brimming with sadness. Rahul remembered the first time they had met. It was this zeal to help others that had brought them together in the first place. Had Uncle ji not twisted his ankle on the railway platform on that fateful day, Rahul and Aditi wouldn't have crossed each other's paths. And then a thought struck his mind; Uncle ji's son Akshat had battled COVID-19 just a month back. If his blood group matched with Arun's then he would surely be able to donate his plasma to Arun. Rahul had found another straw of hope to hold onto. He immediately called Akshat. The phone kept on ringing but there was no answer. Rahul didn't know how to control his emotions. Every second that was ticking away was making him restless and leaving him hopeless. The helplessness one feels on not being able to do anything for a loved one who is slowly drifting away can only be felt and not expressed. The phone beeped. It was Manjeet. He had been able to get the oxygen cylinder filled and was on his way to the hospital. Rahul was ecstatic. Rahul was hoping that now Akshat would soon return his call. He received that call half an hour later. Akshat was ready to donate plasma. Rahul was overjoyed. It was a sign from above that things were falling in place for Arun. They had finally been able to arrange plasma as well as oxygen for Arun. Rahul crossed his fingers and silently thanked God in his heart.

Anjali was sitting on a chair outside the ICU. Hanuman Chalisa was playing on her phone in repeat mode. Arun had a routine of chanting the Hanuman Chalisa every morning. It used to soothe his mind a lot, and provided strength. Anjali had imbibed the habit from him. After an hour or so of listening to the chanting, she called his parents and showed them Arun through a video call from a distance. Even though they couldn't visit him physically, their symbolic presence gave him an immediate boost.

Aditi had been observing all these things. She went to the doctor's room and after getting out of the PPE and sanitising herself, she whispered into Rahul's ears, "Your plan has worked. Ever since Anjali has come here, I have seen a gleam in Arun's eyes that was completely missing. All thanks to you."

Rahul knew that the worst part of this illness is that it breaks human contact. He had insisted on having Anjali in the hospital because he perceived this as the only way to make Arun look forward to being alive. "Anjali has already completed her vaccination schedule, so I am pretty sure about her safety also," Rahul added.

Aditi cautioned Rahul. "You have to encourage Anjali to never be lenient with the necessary precautions. She might be tempted to let her guard down but we will have to be very vigilant about it. Even after being fully vaccinated, many doctors have succumbed to the disease."

Rahul agreed with her and looked at her with eyes full of love. It had been a very long day and there was no respite in view. He didn't want to burden Aditi with his feelings now, when she was already worried. Aditi was surprised at this development. Of late, she had become accustomed to his glares and the way he used to nitpick and fight with her. She had forgotten how she used to savour his loving glances. She cherished the moment and buried it deep in her heart, to make it sempiternal.

Akshat reached the hospital at 12:30 a.m. Rahul went down to the blood bank with him. After taking the sample, the technician told them that the report would take some time to come. After Rahul left for the blood bank, Aditi received an SOS from the ICU. Arun's oxygen saturation levels were dipping. She instructed the junior doctor who was on duty to increase the pressure of oxygen but it did not seem to have any effect. She waited for some time before asking him to increase it further. It was a desperate wait. Anjali was traumatised as she witnessed Arun's falling saturation levels. She was hoping that increasing the pressure of the oxygen would be sufficient to improve his saturation levels but it was not working. Aditi asked the staff nurse to make him do 'proning' which he was very reluctant to do as it was very painful for him. In the meantime, she slipped into a PPE kit and made a dash for the ICU. Arun was too weak to even look at her. Aditi took over from the nurse and made him lie down on his belly. She checked for the pressure of oxygen and asked him to try taking deep breaths. Arun could make excuses with the nurse but Aditi's presence gave him confidence and he quietly abided by her instructions. Some ten minutes later, as the oximeter touched 91, Aditi heaved a sigh of relief. As per the norms of the government, every hospital had been given a tablet and a person had been appointed to operate it. His task was to help the patients connect with their families via video calls and also to connect the patients with doctors in times of need. Aditi instructed Rahul to keep a tab on Arun and keep her updated.

While Rahul and Akshat were waiting for the blood samples to be matched so that they could proceed further, Aditi was trying to ameliorate Arun's condition. Rahul was oblivious of what Arun was going through. The most common problem that the doctors were facing with the younger COVID patients was that they were succumbing to heart attacks despite being put on anticoagulants and blood thinners. The virus was taking its toll despite the patients' high immunity levels without any discrimination between male, female, or old, young or any other category. It was striking some in the lungs and some others in the gut. The unpredictable course of warfare was leaving the doctors baffled. It was Arun's eighth day of fever and Aditi was very concerned about him. The infection would go away on its own by the 14th day like any other viral infection but the devastation it would cause in the body by that time was a major cause of concern. Aditi was desperately waiting for Akshat's reports to come so that they could infuse plasma into Arun's blood stream.

The report came at two in the morning just as Manjeet reached the hospital with the oxygen cylinder. Thankfully, even the hospital had received enough stock of oxygen by then because of timely intervention by the district administration. The hospital staff had also been working 24x7 in the wake of the pandemic. The immense value of human life had been understood by everyone in this dreadful phase. Nobody had witnessed such a macabre dance of death in their life span. It had been more than two centuries when such a pandemic had been reported which had wiped out a sizable portion of the human population. The 21st century humans had considered themselves to be beyond such a pandemic. The advances in scientific knowledge didn't let them believe that a microscopic virus would crash their dreams like a house of cards. Terrifying tales of miseries were reported in each and every district of the country. This was beyond human endurance.

Their samples matched and the transfusion was immediately arranged. Aditi was hopeful that Arun would show signs of improvement by the next day itself. As everyone decided to call it a day at 6 a.m. in the morning, they prayed to the Almighty to show some visible improvement in Arun's health by the next day. Rahul advised Anjali to get some sleep and come back whenever she was comfortable. She flatly refused to budge from Arun's side and both of them had tears in their eyes as they looked at Arun whose breathing seemed to be very laboured. Anjali and Rahul tried catching some sleep in the waiting area of the hospital while Aditi was in the doctor's room. All three got disturbed sleep.

Arun's symptoms weren't improving. Rahul always kept himself updated about the latest technologies or medicines being used around the world to treat COVID. He asked Aditi about the drug cocktail—the monoclonal antibodies that had been given emergency use permission in India. Aditi had already started gathering information about it but she wasn't sure if the same would be useful for Arun. She told Rahul that she planned to consult other senior doctors on Arun's case and the possible administration of Casirivimab and Imdevimab to Arun. Rahul had read that people had shown remarkable recovery and were discharged within 12 hours of having been injected with the antibodies. Even the American president had received the same treatment and had recovered successfully despite having several comorbidities. Rahul wanted something similar done to save Arun. All he could do was persevere by his friend's side, provide everything that the doctors needed for his treatment, and have faith in the Almighty to improve his friend's condition.

Aditi discussed the case with her HOD Dr Poonam, and senior consultants Dr Namita and Dr Yogita, and found that the treatment was not tenable in Arun's case. His disease had advanced to the severe stage and all they could do was increase the steroid dosage and give him symptomatic treatment while keeping a tab on his vitals. Rahul felt disheartened but he also knew that the doctors were the best judge and he couldn't bring in his 'google knowledge' to treat his friend.

Ten days went past in a flurry. Hospital, office and the godown consumed Rahul's life in those days. Arun was critical but recovering under the care of competent doctors. It was the beginning of June and he had managed to supply Mr Bajaj's first order on time. He decided to give the news to Arun, who had been shifted to the non-COVID ward in the morning and could then be visited by friends and family. He received a pleasant surprise as he entered the room. For the first time in over a fortnight, he saw Arun sitting and eating food on his own. Anjali was by his side and Aditi was also present in the separate single room allotted by the hospital. Arun was more excited than Rahul. He giggled like a kid when he saw Rahul's face. Even though Arun had lost more than 10 kgs and the road to complete recovery seemed long, yet the thought that the two ladies present in the room had given their everything to save his friend filled him with gratitude towards them. If anything would have happened to Arun, Rahul would have been devastated. Aditi told him that Arun would be discharged within a few days but special care would have to be taken in giving him nutritious food, timely medication and proper exercise. Rahul assured her that he would do everything as per her instructions.

****

As the number of COVID cases had declined, life began to return back to normalcy. While the central government announced the centralised vaccine procurement programme, the Delhi state government announced the 'Jahan Vote, Wahan Vaccination' campaign. It had been a month since Arun had returned home. All the friends were sitting together sipping hot ginger tea when Arun's parents rang the doorbell. Arun was overjoyed beyond words. He hadn't seen them in person ever since the pandemic had clutched India in its deadly grip. Rahul felt greatly relieved on seeing his parents. It was taking a toll on him to manage the business singlehandedly while taking care of Arun alongside. Judging by the suitcases his parents were carrying, Rahul was sure that they had come to stay with them for some time. He touched their feet, took blessings and went in to make 'Rahul special' ginger tea for them.

Rahul had been unable to express his love and desires to Aditi ever since the day he had admitted his mistakes to himself. With Arun's health issues being the centre of concern, he had never had any solitary moment with Aditi, and he had not been able to confess to her how deeply apologetic he felt about the mistakes he had made. One fine day, he dressed his best and reached the hospital when he knew Aditi's shift was about to get over. He entered the doctor's room and was looking around for Aditi when the head nurse observed him. She smiled at the lovelorn young man clasping a bouquet of fresh roses in his hands desperately looking for his lady love. The sprint in his step and the sparkle in his eyes reminded the elderly nurse of her youthful days and the thrill of being in love for the very first time. She blushed at the memory itself. She easily perceived Rahul's restlessness and told him that Dr Aditi had just gone to the washroom to freshen up. Rahul sat down and waited for her.

Aditi was astounded to see Rahul waiting in the doctor's room. His perfectly coiffed hair accentuated his looks and his carefully selected attire highlighted his features. The red rose bouquet in Rahul's hand told her all that Rahul wanted to convey. She looked at herself and was aghast. She didn't want him to see her in her crumpled attire and in all her unattractive glory. But she didn't have any other choice. She slowly walked up to him and waved at him. The first thing he told Aditi was how pretty she looked. She asked him not to embarrass her but when she looked into his deep expressive eyes she blushed as she knew that he meant what he had said. She was deeply touched and realised that her clothes and her looks didn't really matter to him. His eyes spoke a language that only her heart could understand and she was exhilarated. And then Rahul went down on his knee to give her the bouquet and his eyes looked endearingly at her. Aditi took the bouquet in her own hands and caressed the fresh roses slowly while hoping to hear the very words from Rahul that she always wanted to.

"Maybe today is not the day." thought Aditi as Rahul raised himself up and muttered, "I'm sorry." Aditi smiled faintly. She had already forgiven him.

As the days rolled by, Rahul toiled in his office to cover up for the time lost during the second wave. He did not want to disturb Arun, as for the latter, rest was of utmost importance. Arun's parents were taking good care of him to help him recover from the long COVID. The presence of Arun's parents in the house brought immense relief for Rahul who could finally pay attention to the pending office work without having to worry about Arun anymore. Some relief came Aditi's way too when the second wave of COVID subsided and her duty hours relaxed. Now she too could finally focus on the NEET exam scheduled for 11 September 2021. It was a tough call for her to begin preparations for the exam right after the macabre events of the pandemic. But her dream of studying Paediatrics was the force that kept her going.

Rahul thought it better not to disturb Aditi at this crucial juncture and let her focus on her exam. Thus, everyday, after the office hours he was left to his own meditations. Earlier he used to chat with Aditi for hours while driving back from the office. Now he would silently drive down the road taking note of the things on the way.

In the month of September, Rahul was there when Aditi appeared for the exam. He waited outside the exam centre for hours, and when Aditi came out beaming with hope for a favourable outcome she found Rahul waiting for her with a couple of burgers and her favourite cup of cold coffee.

Aditi went gung-ho about the exam while gobbling up the burger hungrily. Rahul watched her, smiling at her childlike excitement. The pleasure of Aditi's company was all that he desired.

After the exam Aditi packed her bags from the hostel and went to her house. To her surprise, her father had planned a holiday trip to Gangtok. And so Aditi left for Gangtok to spend some quality time with her family. Rahul missed her presence badly. He would find refuge only in the photos that she would share with him. In the humdrum of his life, without Aditi by his side, he too became homesick. Seeing Aditi with her parents in those photos, he too would miss his family.

****

Alongside the avenue, pines and maulshris were proudly swinging in their green glory. Rahul's car was gliding past them on the Prithviraj Road. Every time Rahul passed that way a bit of homesickness would return to haunt him. It reminded him of Gaya and then the memory would evoke a longing to see everyone again; Amma, Baba, Reema, Sugna, Pintu and those streets too where he had spent all his childhood running amok without a care, and the trees that he would climb with Arun to pluck mulberries and mangoes. It had been six months since Arun had recovered from the deadly disease. Although for almost three months he could not contribute much to the business, now he was hale and hearty again. He had taken a lot of the work upon himself so that he could provide Rahul some relief from it. He would often coax Rahul to visit his parents too whom he had not met ever since he stepped into the city. But Rahul had not been able to do so. Not even on Diwali. Though he had planned everything and made up his mind to celebrate Diwali at home, but the increasing workload foiled his plans.

The declining air quality of Delhi had increased the demand for supplies in its wake. Delhi was bearing the brunt of stubble burning in the adjoining states supplemented by vehicular pollution, and pollution caused due to industrial and construction activities. Despite the recurring nature of Delhi's declining air quality situation this time of the year, the whole state machinery failed to tackle it yet again. Rahul got busy arranging for the medical supplies to the clients while consoling himself that he would visit home in the new year, which was only about a month away now. After all, he had assured Amma of coming home soon when she expressed her displeasure for his failure to turn up on Diwali. The expanding business needed him more than ever. Rahul was trying to set everything in order before his visit to Gaya; the release of orders, disbursements, settling of accounts, and sealing of the pending deals. And most importantly he wanted to propose to Aditi in the most romantic way possible before heading back to home. He could then tell Amma about her, and solemnize his relationship with Aditi with the approval of his parents. To him everything appeared settled by now his own business that was experiencing significant upswing and Aditi's career too, as she had cleared the NEET PG exam with flying colours. She was eagerly waiting for her counselling and seat allocation. She was quite hopeful of getting admission in Paediatrics in a medical college in Delhi.

While Rahul was busy making these plans, reports of a new heavily mutated variant of coronavirus had started pouring in from South Africa. The governments were mulling over imposing bans over international flights. The advisories were being issued to people afresh through the media. The Omicron scare was slowly gaining ground around the world. Soon the WHO declared it as a variant of concern. By 6 December 2021, Omicron cases in India went up to 23 and India recorded 8,306 new COVID-19 cases on the same day. Delhi also reported the first case of Omicron infection. Several states stepped up vaccination, surveillance and containment measures again.

Watching the reports flashing across the news channels on the TV screen, Delhi CM urging people not to panic but to wear masks and adhere to COVID-19 protocols, Rahul took a deep breath thinking he already had seen the worst, and nothing could be graver than that. It was as if the subsequent COVID waves had caused a fatigue that numbed his senses so much so that he could not even feel a reaction to anything related to COVID now. He shook all those thoughts away. He hated it when the day would begin with such news reports. Rahul snatched the TV remote from Arun's hands and changed the channel. Arun had become accustomed to it and knew that Rahul did not like it.

But little did he know that destiny had other plans in store for him. After all, the course of life cannot really be dictated simply by one's wishes and desires. The next moment Rahul's phone rang. Both of them looked at the screen anxiously. A call from Dr Ehsan that late at night was enough to send warning bells ringing in their heads. Dr Ehsan needed their support to control the spread of the omicron variant. He did not want it to spiral out of control as the previous waves did. The belligerent virus was unleashing its havoc and ironically the masses were becoming increasingly casual in their approach yet again.

The government launched a vaccination drive for children in the 15-18 year age group. Dr Ehsan wanted people across social groups to participate in the drive and get vaccinated. Awareness was the key to make it a success. Rahul and Arun were his best bet. They had the knack of coming up with innovative ideas to address complex situations. The well disposed duo assured Dr Ehsan of their support.

A few weeks later, the vaccination statistics of their district were staggering. 80% of the youth had been fully vaccinated, much higher than the vaccination figures of other districts. On 14 February 2022, Dr Ehsan congratulated Rahul and broke the news to him that the District Magistrate had decided to honour both Rahul and Arun for their exemplary services during the COVID pandemic.

Rahul was ecstatic but wanted to brush anything associated with COVID away from his mind, especially today when he had asked Aditi out. Today he had planned to open his heart to Aditi in a way he had never done before and also in the way Aditi had always expected him to.

Rahul was very sure of his future with Aditi and wanted his eternity with her to start at the earliest. While he was waiting outside her home, rehearsing in his mind how he would express his love to her, a lady carrying a boy of around a year knocked at his window. She gestured at Rahul to give her money to feed the baby. Rahul found it absolutely difficult to brush aside such people. Especially when he believed he needed all the blessings he could gather. The lady seemed to be from a decent family and not a beggar.

He asked her why she was carrying such a young child like that. The lady broke down and Rahul quickly stepped out of the car to console her. The lady told Rahul that her name was Sujata and her husband used to work as an office boy. He had succumbed to corona in the month of April when the entire nation was battling the second wave. They didn't have any savings and her husband was the only earning member of the family. She had somehow managed for a few months, but now she didn't know how to feed herself and her son and so she had resorted to begging. Rahul empathised with her but also knew that such a situation needed more than that. He told her about the Mukhyamantri COVID-19 Pariwar Aarthik Sahayata Yojana, in which the Delhi government had announced that a sum of ₹ 50,000 ex gratia will be given to every family that lost a member to COVID-19, and an additional ₹ 2,500 per month will be given if the deceased was the sole breadwinner. Rahul found time to get Sujata connected with the team of Dr Ehsan for assistance. Sujata was very grateful to Rahul for this generous gesture and started to walk away. So many schemes are floated across every other day. She had to arrange the next meal for her son and for herself and she didn't want to get into an argument with a stranger over any new scheme that had been floated. Rahul sensed her despair and gave her the sandwiches he had brought for his lunch but couldn't eat because of all the butterflies in his stomach. She unpacked the sandwich and gave it to her son who devoured it in no time. In the meantime, Rahul asked for her details and registered her on the website to claim the benefits of the scheme. He told her that some government official would visit her place soon to complete the formalities. She was extremely grateful to Rahul and went away, blessing him.

Just then Aditi stepped out of her house. She was wearing a sleeveless fuchsia top with body hugging blue jeans. The white fur shrug carelessly thrown over it completed her casual look. Every step she took in her red pencil heels pierced Rahul's heart. As she sat beside him in the car, Rahul's entire being was filled with the vibrant, fruity fragrance of her Burberry perfume. As she settled in the car, her phone buzzed. She wouldn't have taken it but it was from the hospital. The nurse informed her that they had successfully wrapped up the vaccination of 12-14 year olds for the day. It was her responsibility to keep Aditi informed about the number of doses administered and to report if anyone had any adverse reaction to the vaccine. Rahul asked her to leave aside all the cares for the day and be ready for the journey of a life time. He pushed the accelerator hard and Aditi was wondering what to expect next.

She had just seen Sujata walk away from the car. She looked questioningly at Rahul and he told Aditi about Sujata's despair and how he had helped her. Aditi was amazed at this marvellous man who didn't bat an eye before helping anyone out. At a time when humanity had lost its meaning to so many people, Rahul was the torchbearer, the beacon of hope for those who had lost hope from all quarters. Aditi couldn't take her eyes off him. Her soul was flooded with love and she kept staring at him. She touched his black, lustrous hair that he had groomed so well. He was handsome in an understated way; his aquiline nose complemented his high cheekbones and Aditi found herself completely floored by him. Evoking from her sensations she never knew she was capable of feeling, her heart was beating like a hammer hitting against a wall. She dived into the depths of his eyes and could only see pure love. She wanted to come back to the surface but she was drowning in his love. Her soul was aglow in the colours of his love.

Aditi didn't notice when they reached India Gate. Rahul quickly got out and as he opened the door for her, he gently took her hand and helped her alight from the car. Rahul had never seen her look so beautiful. Her sharp contours, sculpted and pared to perfection; her deep-set eyes bright and spell binding as lode stars; the glow on her face and above all the simplicity of her character had tied him to her on a leash. He wanted to bare his heart to her.

Nature was in consonance with their heart's desires and feelings. The sudden drizzling that began was reflective of the love that was permeating them. They didn't seek any shelter under a tree as they wanted to get drenched in each other's love. Several young children came running towards them as they took a turn towards the Raj Path. Rahul had helped them return to their villages during the lockdown earlier and they considered him to be their messiah. Now it was their turn to help Rahul unite with Aditi. The kids took out their self-made musical instruments and formed a circle around them and held up placards 'WILL YOU MARRY ME?' One of them handed Rahul a single red rose. Rahul had never imagined that he would do this. Aditi stood stupefied while Rahul went down on his knee in front of the India Gate and proposed to her...

❑